THE
IMPACT
OF A
SAINT

THE IMPACT

Meetings with Kirpal Singh
and Ajaib Singh, 1963-76

Sant Bani Ashram

OF A SAINT

RUSSELL PERKINS

anbornton, New Hampshire, 1980

Copyright © 1980 by Russell Perkins
Library of Congress Catalog Card No. 80-51959
ISBN: 80-89142-037-1

Second printing, 1989
Third printing, 2001

Photocomposition and printing by
The Sant Bani Press, Tilton, N.H.

To my Guru
who met me and loved me
first as Kirpal
then as Ajaib
from whom this book came
to whom it is returned

In most books, the *I*, or first person, is omitted; in this it will be retained; that, in respect to egotism, is the main difference.

THOREAU: *WALDEN*

Preface

This is a true story. Parts of it may be hard to believe, but they are true all the same. The narrative covers the entire period of my association with my guru, Kirpal Singh; the period of terrible confusion following his physical death in 1974; and the sweet and wonderful way in which I was dragged to the meeting with his successor, Ajaib Singh. It ends with my second trip to Ajaib Singh's ashram, in May 1976. The story of course did not end there; but the many things that have happened since then—the beautiful, very fruitful association with Ajaib Singh, the tremendous expansion of his work, the way in which hundreds of Westerners every year leave civilization behind for a two-week sojourn in his desert ashram, his world tours—may someday find their way into a book of their own: they are too much for this one.

The scope, structure, chapter titles, and length of this book were all strictly laid down for me by Kirpal Singh, and I have done my best to literally obey him.

A few spiritual experiences have been included, with the Master's permission, wherever the narrative made no sense without them. These should not be understood to imply any degree whatever of spiritual competence or "advancement" on my part. Such experiences are, or ought to be, the norm on the spiritual path, and the ultimate goal of the practitioner lies far beyond them. Further, any initiate can testify that if anything is clear to him, it is this: that any spiritual or mystical experience whatever is entirely a matter of grace: it is a gift of the Guru. None of us deserve anything along this line, and if we think we do, we are dead.

I owe a great deal to many people, as the narrative (I hope) makes clear, especially to my family—Judith, Miriam, Eric—for living it with me. But I would be terribly amiss if I did not publicly note my gratitude to Susan Gilb, whose counsel and encouragement—always wise, never failing—was the factor which made it possible for me to obey the Master and write the book. I will always be grateful to her.

RUSSELL PERKINS

Preface to the 1989 Edition

Most of this book was written eleven years ago, in the summer of 1978, although I continued to work on it for two more years. A great great deal has happened since then, and I have given some thought to adding several chapters to bring the story up to date. Nevertheless, it still seems that that should be another book, which may some day get written.

I would like to once again express my profound gratitude and thanks for the infinite protective care and guidance of my Guru, working through the body of Ajaib Singh. Elsewhere I have written: "The story is not over, thank God; it continues, and one thing many of us have learned: the grace of God working through the living Master is full of surprises. To follow the Path . . . is an intensely real roller-coaster ride up and down the mountains of our Self, and at the end of it is more than we dreamed possible." That I have been given the grace of making that ride and beginning to discover what is there seems the greatest gift that anyone could be given.

Rereading this book after a considerable time, it is impossible not to notice its many flaws. I appreciate and need the indulgence of the reader.

R.P.

Table of Contents

List of Illustrations

Frontispiece Sant Kirpal Singh Ji holding Satsang at Sant Bani Ashram, Sanbornton, New Hampshire, October 1972

The numbered pictures are between pages 66 and 67.

THE
IMPACT
OF A
SAINT

Ask, and it shall be given you;
seek, and ye shall find;
knock, and it shall be opened unto you:
For everyone that asketh receiveth;
and he that seeketh findeth;
and to him that knocketh it shall be opened.

MATTHEW 7: 7-8

Whoever seeks the Satguru will surely find Him,
for the Satguru is an incarnation eternally
present on this earth.

SAR BACHAN 2: 208

CHAPTER ONE

In Search of a Master

This is the story of my adventures with two holy men. What is meant by "holy men"? What is holiness? For most of us, it is that which we don't have but unconsciously long for. For the greater part of our lives, the cry of our soul is just there: a long monotonous groan in the depths of our soul, going on so long that we have long since stopped hearing it. Every once in a while it forces its way through and we *have* to hear it—but we can only hear it through whatever hearing apparatus we have developed. If that is deficient, we will pick up one note only and act on that; but if it is whole, we will no longer experience a groan, but an overwhelming symphony—a waterfall, in fact, carrying us with it as it thunders forth our soul's insatiable, desperate, gasping need for holiness.

There are several ways of understanding holiness:

1) Holiness is *going home*—returning to our source. That part of ourselves which wants to return is a part with which we are badly out of touch, so it is difficult for us to hear this. We have to get in touch with our soul in order to understand it. Nevertheless, a holy person, by definition, is either a person who has returned home or who is preoccupied with returning home.

2) *Holiness is wholeness.* By rearranging our sense of "I" and our various faculties so that we become aware of our soul's pain, we begin the process of making ourselves the unity we were born to be.

3

When we first begin to hear the crying of our own soul, the movement toward holiness begins.

Another way of understanding holiness is as a brilliant white light which, as it passes through a prism, divides into many colors: honesty or integrity, love, non-violence, chastity, etc. While it is rare to find human beings who have made themselves fully whole, so that the brilliant white light shines unmistakeably from them, it is not so rare to find human beings in whom one color is manifesting fully. Their lives may be badly flawed in other ways, but if they show us one facet of holiness in practice, they have the power to touch our lives and move us deeply.

The idea of "searching" for God, or for some connection to Him, or for Truth, or whatever, seems odd: "Kabir says, I laugh when I hear the fish in the water is thirsty." Why do we have to search for that which we already have? But most of the searching that we do in our life is just that—looking for something we already have, *but have lost touch with*. No doubt our soul is there—but where? Can we hear it? Searching is another name for learning to listen; for fitting a strand here and a strand there so that gradually, little by little, a symphony emerges—the symphony that is our ultimate Self.

But the first strand is undoubtedly the moan of the starving soul. When we learn to listen to that, the rest follows. And with the first overwhelming awareness that the soul is in agony—that is to say, that *we* are in agony—it becomes very clear that *we need help*.

In my own life, I heard fragments and echoes of my soul's symphony at intervals from a very early age, but I became clever at evading them. One of my earliest memories is of my mother reading *The Wizard of Oz* to me, and afterward taking me to see the movie, which had just come out. This was in 1939, when I was four: both the book and the movie made a tremendous impression on me, and my earliest extended memories are centered on this double experience. I have always loved the story (indeed, all the Oz stories) but it is only as an adult that I came to realize what a powerful parable of the homegoing of the soul that story is, and to speculate on just what degree of influence being exposed to it so vividly so early had on my later life.

Later I was given a comic book based on the Bible (*Picture Stories from the Bible*). I loved it. It was full of stories of people who talked with God, presented as a very natural thing. It struck me as I read it that *this was the norm*—that it was meant for human beings to be on intimate terms with God. I asked my mother about it, and she said that it was like that once, but not any more. I did not argue, but I felt in my heart that it *was* possible, even now.

When I was fourteen, I began to read the Bible. I thought it would be appropriate to begin with the life of Christ, so I started at the beginning of the New Testament. I read with pleasure Matthew's account of Jesus's birth and the visit of the wise men, and then before I knew it, I was into the Sermon on the Mount. I had gone to church and Sunday-school all my life, and had been brought up in a Christian family, but never had I heard anything like this. "Judge not that ye be not judged"—I felt prickles going up the back of my neck. I thought, has *anybody* read this? Then how can society exist? "Blessed are the pure in heart for they shall see God." I thought, is that a promise? And if so, when? The long section on swearing struck me as piercingly beautiful, and I memorized it. But underlying the whole was a sense of the universe which I had never come across once—even though I had associated with Christians all my life. This was bewildering to a fourteen-year-old; the impression that I came away with was that what Jesus had taught had nothing to do with Christianity.

A year or two later I read Thoreau's *Walden* in high school (not *for* high school—it was not assigned—but physically in it) and again the same reaction: I had heard about Thoreau all my life, and everyone spoke of him with respect, not to say veneration. *But no one had ever read him.* Because never in my life had I heard anyone say anything remotely comparable to the things I read in that book. Again I had that feeling of an underlying sense of the universe blocked off from me, but known to Jesus and Thoreau—as though they had been able to grasp its handle, while I was still groping for it; indeed before I read them, I didn't know it was there to grope for.

In 1950, when I was fifteen, Billy Graham came to Boston and conducted a series of revival meetings that were given maximum publicity in the Boston Globe. We were living in New Hampshire and I could not attend personally, but I was fascinated: did these people understand what Jesus was talking about? It seemed to me that they did; certainly something was going on that had to do with the transformation of human life—or so it seemed. Jesus, God, death, the human soul, *mattered.* They occupied a central place in the evangelical consciousness, not pushed into a back corner and forgotten about except when convenient. The sense of urgency and personal concern about the status of one's soul struck me as real and important, and I took evangelicals and their understanding of the Bible very seriously. In due course, on July 11, 1951, at what is now the Evangelical Baptist Church of Laconia, New Hampshire, I was "born again."

I put quotes around that phrase because it has been a very long time since I have believed that what happened to me on that night was what Jesus was talking about when he referred to being "born again."[1] Certainly something real happened: the effort required to propel me forward in front of the whole congregation was enormous, and involved a tremendous emotional release. Despite having attended church for some time, I did not really understand the theology involved; I knew only that God required a public affirmation of my love for and surrender to Him, and of my faith in Christ. I did not grasp the subtler implications of the "vicarious atonement" theory for some time, and when I did I didn't like it. I accepted it reluctantly for a while, then rejected the whole system. By that time (after two years in an evangelical college) I had come to the conclusion that evangelicalism had nothing more to do with Jesus than anything else—perhaps less.

I objected primarily to the grafting of theology on to an experience that is real but indefinable. Whether or not the evangelical "born again" or "salvation" experience is the same thing that Jesus was talking about (and I will explain later why I don't think it is, and what I think Jesus *was* talking about) the fact is that in itself it is an emotional experience that can be very real and satisfying to the convert. But no one would ever know, without an army of ministers, Bible "experts," and older Christians to tell him, that as part and parcel of his conversion he now believed in the Bible as absolutely infallible and inerrant; in a God who created human beings knowing fully well that the vast majority would end up in hell; in a view of the universe which considers it just and right that a loving and merciful God would confer infinite punishment for a finite sin. Later it became clear that no God worth worshiping would act in such a way as to make him morally inferior to his wor-

1. See the third chapter of the Gospel of John.

shipers: if even I could see the injustice in an eternal hell as a response to a few years of struggle, why could not he? It seemed to me that to worship such a God only to save my own skin made me as unworthy as he was.

So I left the evangelical faith in 1954, and I have never regretted it.

In confusion over the falling apart of my faith, I lost interest in religion altogether and my longing for understanding, for something to fill that gigantic hole, was diverted into the theater. I entered Boston University School of Theater Arts in the fall of 1954 and for the next two years studied acting and directing with Alexander Kirkland, Peter Kass, Jose Quintero, and others. I loved it. I got to know Shakespeare and Shaw really well (I had met them both previously) and made the acquaintance for the first time of Ibsen, Brecht, Chekhov, Synge and T.S. Eliot. Eventually I decided that I was better suited for writing than acting, and in the spring of 1956 I left Boston University, although I continued to live in the neighborhood and to maintain contact with many of my friends.

During this period, I read *The Brothers Karamazov* and added Dostoevsky to my list of literary idols (I also read *War and Peace*, but my love for Tolstoy came much later, with a second reading). More and more I thought of myself as a writer, and less and less did I write. Most of my energy went into the way I thought a writer should live—which included heavy drinking, party-going, eventually working as little as possible and "borrowing" money as much as possible, and above all else, talk—endless gallons of talk, flowing flowing flowing into the bars, and when they closed, the all-night restaurants. There is a line from Allen Ginsberg's *Howl*, written about this time, that struck me when I first read it and has remained with me: "We sank all night in the submarine light of Bickford's.'' It didn't seem to us that we were sinking; it seemed to us that we were handling and coming to grips with every possible problem in the universe. But in reality we *were* sinking and floundering in the endless tidal waves of talk.

In the summer of 1956, I spent two months in a cabin on a friend's land in rural New Hampshire (not far from my parents' home) trying to write a novel, and failing. That fall I returned to Boston and began my last year of work as a hospital orderly. As the autumn turned into winter, my old questions and preoccupations began to return, though at first so subtly that I was hardly aware of them. For the first time in about three years, questions about ultimates gradually began to resume their accustomed place. Christmas week, 1956, was the premiere of *The Ten Commandments*, and I went to see it. It is not considered a great movie, I know; but I found it very compelling. The intensely personal nature of Moses' relationship to God moved me deeply. I saw it several times.

On New Year's Day 1957 I was working as a call orderly at the New England Baptist Hospital. I was alone in the operating room all day; few if any calls came to me. I did my best to sort out the thoughts and feelings that had been building up. Certain things fell into place: I saw that either there was such a thing as Absolute Truth or there was not; that if there was, then I knew with an overwhelming clarity that I *had* to find it; and that since if there was no Absolute, it didn't matter what I did, then why not act as though there was? I used the word "overwhelming"; although to write about it requires many words and makes it seem like it was a reasoned out conclusion, in fact the entire realization occurred in a split second. The reasoning came afterward. From that day to this, I have understood that my main work is to find Absolute Truth; I am not speaking of others. It was a personal understanding and has remained so. Several times in my life I have heard unmistakably the voice of my soul; this was the first, and from this all else followed. Still there was the problem of how. I had made an internal commitment of the profoundest seriousness, and for the first time in my life I felt at peace with the universe. But what to do next? I had no idea. But suddenly the words from the Sermon on the Mount that had seared themselves on my soul years before came into my mind: "Ask, and it shall be given you; seek, and ye shall find; knock, and it shall be opened unto you: For everyone that asketh receiveth; and he that seeketh findeth; and to him that knocketh it shall be opened. Or what man is there of you, whom if his son ask bread, will he give him a stone? . . . If ye then being evil, know how to give good gifts unto your children, how much more shall your Father which is in heaven give good things to them that ask him?"[2] I had never understood these words before; as with so many of Jesus's words, there is no room for them in the traditional Christian theology. But now it was as though Jesus himself was speaking directly to my innermost essence, and these words sustained me and gave me hope through the coming months. I realized that since I had made my commitment to the universe and *meant* it, it was up to the universe to show me what to do next; I also realized that while this seemed wildly, ridiculously presumptuous when put in these words, it was nonetheless *exactly what Jesus meant.* And so it happened, in my experience, that the promise was kept and it was shown to me without a doubt that Jesus's words mean exactly what they seem to mean.

    The day after I had made my commitment, a friend of

2. Matthew 7:7-11.

mine gave me a book, saying, "Here—I think you ought to read this." The book was *A New Model of the Universe,* by P.D. Ouspensky, and I had never read a book like it; each paragraph was a new revelation. It was the book I needed, I saw that right away; it gave me the theoretical knowledge I needed to implement my search. Here for the first time I read about the idea of "esotericism"—that there is a knowledge having to do with the attainment of Truth; that it has to be searched for, but it can be found; and that there are people living on earth now who have done this, and they are the ones who are to be sought—because, once found, they can help us become what they are. In his chapter on the Superman, Ouspensky wrote that when we search for the Superman outside of us, we find him within us; and that when we search for him within, we find him without. That passage made a very powerful impression on me.

While I was reading this book, I mentioned to a good friend of mine—a poet—the lines along which I was thinking, and he replied that he had had a similar experience and was also searching for higher things. This was amazing, because we had been friends for a year and a half and roommates for three months and never once had this kind of thing been discussed between us. One day later he introduced me to another young man whom he had just met; this man was also searching for truth. And so it went; in a very short time a group of us ranging at various times between four and eight had pooled our resources and our insights and were searching for truth together.

We were very serious and our search was two-pronged, utilizing both books and real live people. In order to understand the nature of our undertaking, it is necessary to forget the developments of the past twenty years (I am writing in 1978) and go back to 1957, when words like *guru* and *karma* were almost completely unknown; when nobody outside of the Seventh Day Adventist Church was a vegetarian; when esoteric and mystical ideas were almost totally confined to so-called "occult" circles: the world of psychics, astrologers, spiritualists, at that time almost exclusively middle-aged and middle-class, and generally considered something of a "lunatic fringe" by respectable intellectuals. Our search was a vastly different project then than it would be today: we were hampered by a scarcity of resources, a lack of anything promising to search among, whereas today the opposite is true: the seeker has to make his way through a luxuriant underbrush of often conflicting ideas before reaching what he is really after—unless he settles for less.

Shortly after meeting my new friends and establishing ourselves as a serious group with real aims, one of them suggested that Ouspensky's *In Search of the Miraculous* would be much more helpful to me than *A New Model of the Universe* had been. He was right. *New Model,* while rich in concepts and seed ideas, had been disappointingly poor in specifics; *In Search of the Miraculous* was apparently a word-for-word transcript of a series of lectures given by G.I. Gurdjieff (whom I discovered for the first time) and specifics was what it was rich in. For the first time in my search I read the authentic words of a genuine contemporary teacher of real knowledge and stature, and the effect was shattering. I became obsessed with the book; I thought about it constantly; I dreamed about it. It had the ring of truth, and I heard it. Through this book I understood what an "esoteric school" was: a group of students learning how to transform and transcend themselves and realize their full potentiality by working and studying under a teacher *who has already done it.* I read for the first time that all human beings are asleep, that they were unable to "do" or "act," but they could only react; that they were at the mercy of outer circumstances and stimuli, and their own involuntary longings and fears; that they were in fact "machines" rather than human beings, and as long as this condition persisted one could not speak of psychology but only of mechanics. A terrible picture of humanity indeed! Yet, looking at my own life and the lives of those around me, once all the sentiment and wishful thinking were swept away, it was self-evidently true. Besides, there was a way out: people who had come to understand the true state of affairs could, by working together and submitting themselves to the instruction and discipline of a competent teacher—not just intellectually competent—develop within themselves the capability of reversing the process, waking up, acting instead of reacting, and rising above the whole mess.

Simultaneously with our reading, we personally explored every person or group in the Boston area who gave any indication of *knowing more than we did.* This was the phrase we used as a criterion, and of course we meant it in a very specific way. We meant that whoever we went to should have achieved something real, but we did not demand that it be much: if it was more than we had achieved, we could learn something. We also decided that we would examine each person or group with an absolutely open mind *as long as we were with them,* and analyze and reflect only afterwards. In this way we would have the maximum opportunity to learn.

But we didn't learn much. My memories of those wintry Bostonian days and nights are a curious mixture of intense excitement and anticipation on the one hand, and a series of really ludicrous disappointments on the other. Drab, almost sordid psychic meetings on second floors of slum buildings; negotiations with a five-foot tall, very plump Rosicrucian lady over how much she would charge us for our lessons (which never came off, for some reason I have forgotten); a meeting with a small, hand-rubbing Spiritualist minister and his large, formidable wife, both beautifully dressed, in their Back Bay apartment, during which they informed us of their life's ambition: that their spirit contact would someday blow on the trumpet that was sitting on their living-room floor.

Yet in the midst of the struggle through these dead ends, a blast of hope almost overwhelmed us. It came, again, in the form of a book: *Autobiography of a Yogi* by Paramhansa Yogananda. Anyone who has read this book will surely agree that it is one of the most spectacular of all spiritual books, and it revolutionized our whole search, primarily by introducing a new word in our vocabulary: India. After reading a few pages, I knew as certainly as I had ever known anything that what I was searching for was in India; and I knew that what I was searching for was a Guru.

We read the book to each other in the restaurants and coffee houses of Boston, lingering over cups of coffee as long as we dared in one place, then changing to another. If friends came by, we forced them to listen. Here I learned for the first time in any detail of the ideas of *Karma* and reincarnation; I understood what was meant by *Maya* or "illusion"; I heard for the first time the names of Kabir and Nanak, as well as made the acquaintance of hundreds of spiritual personalities—Eastern and Western—who jumped off the pages in a blaze of light; and above all, beginning with the very first sentence of the book, grasped the value of initiation and the supreme importance of the "disciple-guru relationship." When I think back of the effect that book had on me—of the hope that it brought; the worlds it opened up; the encouragement that it gave—I realize that I owe its illustrious author an immense debt.

Of all the figures so vividly presented in the book, the one who spoke to me most directly was also the most elusive. In fact, the average reader could be pardoned for doubting if he existed at all. Certainly many of my friends doubted it—those on whom I forced a reading of his adventures. I am referring, of course, to Babaji, the thousand-year old Himalayan yogi who was Yogananda's guru's guru's guru, and who was reputed to be living in the mountains still,[3] pursuing a miraculous way of life with a small band of disciples, which included (according to the book) two Americans. Two Americans! Oh, wow! How I longed to be the third American admitted to that little group! Somewhere in my heart rose a firm commitment not to take anyone as a Guru who was of less stature than Babaji. It was a real vow, and I lived up to it.

Some time after I read *Autobiography of a Yogi* I visited my family in New Hampshire. On the train back to Boston I reflected on my experiences of the past months, and as I thought over all the people I had met and the books I had read, the ways in which my life had changed and the understanding I had gained, a tremendous wave of longing came over me, and with all my heart and soul and strength I wanted a Guru. I prayed to Babaji, "Please, please lead me to a Guru; I would like it to be You, but if that's not possible, to Someone not less great." It was the first time in my life that I had prayed with my whole be-

3. Although Babaji has since been identified as Hariakhan Baba, who indisputably exists, this identification has been challenged by some, including a friend of mine who claims to have met the real Babaji personally.

ing, and that prayer was heard: but I was not answered right away. As if the effort to get that far had exhausted me, I went back to sleep: I got involved with a girl, I put in a lot of effort to get my merchant seaman's card, and I forgot not *all* about my search, because what had happened remained with me—but *mostly* about it. It ceased to be the primary reality in my life.

The first hint of awakening came one evening in September 1957. I was walking with a friend when I met one of the persons I had been seeking with. I had not seen him for several months. When he saw me, he pulled me aside, and said, "We've run across something that looks pretty good. Are you still interested?" I said politely that I was, and he gave me the place and time of, apparently, some kind of meeting, which I promptly forgot.

About one month later, in late October, another friend who had been in our group came to see me in my apartment. He didn't waste any time. "We've come across the real thing, and we think you ought to be a part of this too." I was polite but distant. "I'm not interested in anyone unless he's as high as Babaji." My friend leaned forward, looked at me steadily, and said with absolute conviction, "This man is higher than Babaji." Suddenly I was jolted awake—my heart skipped several beats, and I said wonderingly, "How can that be? Is he 900 years old?" My friend laughed. "No," he said, "He's not. But that's not the criterion. This man is a *Satguru*—a Master of Masters—the very highest Master there is." Satguru! I had never heard *that* word before. "What is his name?" "His name is Kirpal."

Kirpal! The very first time I heard that name—how many millions of times since? I was trembling and wide awake, but not yet fully believing—why should I have been? But some part of me knew very well what was going on. My friend promised to come and take me personally to the next meeting, and I agreed to go. He left me with a new name to roll in my mind—and I did. I thought about little else.

I was working as a door-to-door salesman and hating it at that time, and a few nights later, more stress-ridden than usual, I felt weak and faint. I remember stumbling down a flight of stairs and huddling over a toilet seat somewhere, all the time repeating, "Kirpal—Kirpal—Kirpal—Kirpal." The name seemed right to me: it gave me joy and peace to repeat it; and it seemed as though I were calling on an *old friend*. Somehow I got through that night, and I felt grateful to this Kirpal—I had not yet even seen his picture—for helping me.

On Monday night my friend arrived as promised, and we went to my first Satsang, which is what the followers of Kirpal called their meetings. These Satsangs were held then in a little Vedanta Chapel at 202 Commonwealth Avenue in Back Bay, and the first thing that struck me as I entered the room was a huge picture of Ramakrishna, a nineteenth-century Indian Saint whom I had come to love and respect through my reading. On the surface, his picture had nothing whatever to do with the Satsang; it was there because of the Vedanta group that used the Chapel also. But the sight of it was tremendously reassuring to me and gave me a sense of continuity. Then I saw the picture of Kirpal. I stared at it for several seconds, and all I can say about my first reaction to the picture of my Guru is, *that it was no surprise*. I do not mean that it came as a great emotional recognition; it was not like that at all. It is just that it was no surprise; I said, mentally, "Of course, that is the way he looks." And I felt happy.

When I looked around the room, I noticed several friends

from my seeking days, including the young woman who later became my wife—Judith Weinberg. Altogether about fifteen people probably—the ones who I did not know were all older than I, including the Group Leader, a motherly woman from Roslindale who, then and always, treated me with great kindness. The meeting included a lot of reading, most of which I didn't understand although there were ideas I was certainly familiar with, and a half-hour meditation, which was pleasant but unconclusive. After it was over, we—the young people, plus a few others, including Wava, the Group Leader—retired to a nearby Hayes-Bickford's, where a great deal of information was given me at once—more that I could comfortably assimilate. I learned that the Master's full name was Kirpal Singh; that he had been brought up in the Sikh religion of India; that he was 63 years old at that time; and that he had visited Boston for a few days just two years previously, at which time most of the people who had been present at the meeting had been "initiated" and had in that way become his disciples. I learned that there was a special esoteric practice to be initiated into—it was called *Shabda Yoga* or *Sant Mat*, they told me—and that I also could be initiated, but first I had to be a vegetarian for at least three months. A vegetarian! That stopped me. In all my readings I had never noticed the vegetarian idea connected with mysticism (although of course, as I realized later, this was due to my own carelessness: Yogananda, for example, was a vegetarian and specifically mentions it in *Autobiography of a Yogi*). Besides I had only met two vegetarians in my life (one of them a black Seventh-Day Adventist who had worked with me as an orderly; the other was Judith, my future wife, who had become a vegetarian from inner conviction while still in high school). The idea of me becoming a vegetarian did not

fit in with any notions I had about my "image," and I
didn't like it. I asked, "Why?" and I was told that the lives
of animals are worth something in the eyes of God, Who
also made them, and that killing and/or eating any form of
animate life causes heavy karmic reaction and stands in the
way of successful meditation. This answer was plausible
enough in the light of the little that I already knew, but I still
didn't like it and I was far from convinced. (Much later I
came across the Buddha's comment in *The Surangama
Sutra* which sums up the teaching perfectly: "If anyone is
trying to practice meditation and is still eating meat, he is
just like a man who is putting his hands over his ears and
shouting and then complains that he cannot hear anything.")

Other things that were explained to me that night suited
me much more; a lot of it was familiar. The ideas of Karma
and Reincarnation, for example, had figured in many of the
books I had read, especially Yogananda; so the image of the
soul taking birth in body after body while carrying with it
always the effects of its actions (the totality of which,
"good" or "bad," is called *Karma*) gave me no trouble at
all. Neither did the concept of the Satguru as a God-sent being whose primary purpose was to free us from this endless
series of rebirths, show us what our real possibilities were,
and help us to realize them. But *how* he did this was both
new to me and very appealing: for the first time in my life I
heard about the Sound Current. For the first time in my
life; yet, as I listened, I knew that I had heard it all before,
long ago, and that I was rediscovering something that I had
always known but had forgotten.

The "Sound Current" is a rough English translation of
the Sanskrit word *Shabda* and its modern Hindi equivalent,
Shabd (pronounced something like "shubbud"); it is a
poor translation but no better alternative has yet been sug-

gested. It is poor because it is inadequate. The concept or fact that the term represents is tremendous: God is seen as Absolute, indescribable, inconceivable, unreachable: the only way He can be described at all is to say that He is an Ocean of Love. And what is called the Sound Current or (sometimes) the "Word" is a tidal wave of that ocean, manifesting as Light and Sound on different levels in different ways, and ultimately projecting Itself as the created Universe and as all individual persons within that Universe —from the personal God Himself to the lowest form of microscopic life. ("In the beginning was the Word, and the Word was with God, and the Word was God . . . All things were made by him; without him, nothing was made that was made . . . In him was life; and the life was the light of men.")[4] Therefore, if any individual could penetrate deeply enough within himself he would eventually find the Sound Current there, and ultimately the Ocean from which the Current came. Such a person, who has become one with the "Word" or the essence of the Universe, is called a Satguru; and from our point of view it may be unclear as to whether he has become one with the Word or the Word has become one with him. ("And the Word was made flesh, and dwelt among us" . . .[5]) Such a Satguru continues to live on in the world, but only to help others achieve what he has achieved; that is his work. He does that by showing those who want his help how to contact the Sound and Light within themselves and eventually reach the absolute, the Ocean of Love.

It was a supremely breathtaking view of the universe, and I took it seriously from the beginning. I did not necessarily accept it all at once—it was too much for me; but I certainly

4. John 1:1-4
5. John 1:14

respected it. I noted, for example, that while Light and Sound were the primal projections or manifestations of God, His essence would *have* to be love. It followed that a Satguru or a Master would be an incarnation of love. This was certainly how his disciples viewed him, and my inclination was to agree; but of course I had little enough to go on that first night: a subjective reaction to his name, his picture, and some of his words. How did I know anything? And I did not *want* to give up eating meat.

But I did. It didn't happen overnight, but it happened. For about six weeks I marked time: I continued to attend Satsang, I studied Kirpal Singh's writings (which in those days consisted of a few pamphlets; none of his books in English had been published yet), and I let the teachings roll around in my mind. I made no changes in my life other than that. I studied carefully his writings on Karma, which I already knew something about from Yogananda and others, because the teaching on diet was closely bound up with Karma. Kirpal Singh taught, as we have seen, that all life is one, a projection or manifestation of the Word; that to kill, especially to eat, any form of life that is animate or conscious (or is an embryo form of such life) is a serious crime against less-developed children of God; we are, in other words, not supposed to build our bodies on the pain and suffering of others. He also taught that while it was also a crime, ultimately, to kill and eat plants, that we had no choice while in the physical world—to maintain our bodies we had to eat *something*; and the Karma or penalty incurred for killing plants was not so heavy as to prevent us from meditating and penetrating through to our essence. Because, really, the justification for vegetarianism was practical: to eat meat prevented us from meditating effectively and finding that which we wanted to find. If we wanted to meditate effectively and reach our goal, we had to stop eating meat. Very simple. Very logical. But I didn't like it. Intellectually, I could see it; but it didn't connect with anything inside me. And I didn't want to make such a major change without an inner conviction.

I went home to New Hampshire for Thanksgiving, as was my habit; and on Thanksgiving Day we had, as usual, a turkey. My parents tended to make an elaborate ritual over their Thanksgiving turkey, and I had always thought it a lot of fun—as well as enjoying the turkey. But on this occasion the pattern broke: as I was looking at the turkey lying on the dish just before my father began carving it, my perspective consciously shifted (that is to say, I *felt* it shifting) just a little bit, and I saw very clearly that what was lying there on the plate was not delicious food for me, but a corpse—the ruins of something that had once enjoyed pleasure and felt pain even as I did, and that had been of infinite worth in the eyes of God. I saw this in a split second—in much less time than it takes to write about it—and, while I reluctantly ate the turkey that day, it was the last time: the next morning I vowed to become a vegetarian. I did not eat meat again.

That winter I lived through what might be called a final orgy of "beatnik-ism." Knowing that I would be initiated soon and that demands of responsibility and moral living would be made on me, I quit my job and lived as a bum for several months. This was not the first time I had done this, and it was not the last: once more after my initiation I would go through a bout of this disease. Knowing myself as I do, and observing what has happened to many of my friends who were temperamentally like me, I feel that it is only due to grace that I did not end up on Skid Row. My inclination and aptitude toward this kind of life were very pronounced; they were eradicated with difficulty, but they were eradicated, and for that I can only thank God.

Toward the end of this period—just after I had pulled out of the inertia and gotten a job and an apartment, in late March—I was given, by the grace of God, an actual first-hand experience of the greatness of this particular Master. I was neither expecting it nor desiring it; I was at peace with myself, the decision having been made and the turmoil over. In those days Satsang closed with a half-hour meditation, to which everybody, initiated or not initiated, was welcome—and fairly detailed instructions were given (this was before Kirpal Singh had clarified his wishes on this matter). I always participated in the meditations and enjoyed them, although nothing had ever happened—I had seen nothing, heard nothing, experienced nothing. But then I didn't expect to—I wasn't initiated, after all—so it didn't bother me much.

But on this particular night, just after Wava had put us into meditation, I experienced a calmness and peace that went far beyond anything I had experienced before. I became completely immersed in it and lost all track of time, so that I have no idea how much time had gone by when I became aware that *something was going to happen.* I don't know how I knew this, but I did. Suddenly I was looking into a long, long tunnel made of the most beautiful golden light; it was as though I was standing at one end of the tunnel, looking down it toward the other end. Far away in the distance at the other end of the tunnel I could see a figure moving—a very tiny figure, because it was very far away. I couldn't take my eyes off it—I was completely fascinated by that little figure *moving towards me.* As I watched, it came closer and grew bigger, and finally I was able to make out the features of Kirpal Singh, so often seen in photographs. Slowly, but with increasing speed, he came closer and closer; I was able to observe in minute detail his walk and the way he stood. His hands were hanging by his sides, palms toward me, and on his face was the most beautiful, loving, compassionate smile that I had ever seen—the knowledge of the whole universe was in that smile. Closer and closer he came, walking on the Light (although I also understood that all the Light I was seeing was in reality coming from him); smiling on me all the while till I thought he was going to walk right into me; but just as he loomed so large in my inner vision that everything else was blotted out the Group Leader called us out of meditation and I lost it.

The impact of that experience was almost more than I could bear; it almost shattered me. I had never had an experience remotely like it in my whole life, and suddenly I was forced to treat as a reality that which I had been treating as an abstraction. The realness of the Path I had chosen to follow was forced on me, as it were; I had had my nose rubbed in glory.

About six weeks later, on May 11, 1958, six persons were initiated into the Shabd Yoga by a representative of Kirpal Singh in Boston. Five of them, including my future wife, Judith, and myself, had been fellow-seekers after Truth since the year before. Once again Jesus's words, "Seek and ye shall find," had proven true; our Father does *not* give us a stone if we are hungry for bread. The Universe keeps the promises it makes.

CHAPTER TWO

Meetings With The Master

1. Before He Came

Five years passed between my Initiation and my first physical meeting with my Master; five difficult, interesting, vigorous, but in terms of the Path, futile years. My Initiation had been satisfying, although my meditation experiences were considerably less spectacular than the astral meeting with the Master described above. Still I had been given a contact with the Light and Sound, I found meditation both easy and enjoyable, and I certainly did make progress of a sort, in that my connection with the inner Light and Sound grew stronger, and my awareness of them more acute, daily. My meditations were so easy, in fact, that I took them for granted and forgot altogether that it was the Master who was making these things happen. I became careless about the disciplinary requirements I had promised to observe: I resumed drinking alcohol, although I had agreed not to; I was careless about the dietary prohibitions; and I largely ignored the chastity requirement, mainly because I didn't understand it and resented it. In fact I used the occasion of my marriage as an excuse for a long period of intense sensual satisfaction, during which I grew more and more politically oriented and eventually stopped meditating completely.

The period of my non-meditation was exactly two years: September 1959 to September 1961. During this period many essential things happened: my two children were born; after moving around the country, we eventually settled down in Sanbornton, New Hampshire, the same town I had been brought up in; and after some more bouts with ir-responsibility, I learned the trade of a printer, and got a steady job. But I had forgotten all about the Path and the Master.

One afternoon in September 1961 I was working on a paper-cutter at the print-shop when the thought came to me completely unexpectedly: "Suppose I went back on the Path? What would it be like?" I began thinking, as I worked, of all of the adjustments and accommodations I would need to make before such a thing could happen; at first it seemed impossible, but by the end of the afternoon, I knew that it had already happened, in spite of me: I was go-ing back on the Path. I went home and told Judith and she was astounded; she did not share my feelings then but she did a little later.

The next morning I got up early and sat for medita-tion—the first time in two years. I assumed that it would be as easy as it had been before I had stopped. I got a bitter lesson indeed—one of the bitterest I had ever gotten up to that time. I sat with my eyes closed and saw nothing what-soever—no Light at all. I listened for the Sound, and there was dead silence. With one great rush I understood the enormity of what I had done: I had been given the greatest of gifts and I had thrown it away. Tears of self-recrimination and self-pity flooded my eyes as I recalled how easy it had been and how thoroughly I had taken for granted that precious gift. I understood very well that now I would have to work hard and struggle in order to regain that which I had lost.

That day I wrote a letter to the Master. I worked very hard over it, as I was aware that I had not been worthy of what he had given me, and I wanted to impress him. I mailed the letter, and a week or so later there was a letter from him in the mailbox. I was amazed: a week! It took usually a month for letters to get to the Master and back. What could this mean? I read the letter, and it was clear that he was not replying to my letter at all; he had written me without me writing him—a very unusual circumstance. Reflecting further, I realized that he *must have written the letter about the time I had decided to come back on the Path*—that his attention had been directed toward me at that time. It was the first instance in my life of the Protection of the Master, but by no means the last.

The days continued and so did my struggles with meditation. What had once been ridiculously easy was painfully difficult, and I usually did not sit for more than a half-hour. After a few months, I did begin to hear the Sound again, but the Light was kept from me (except for one isolated but joyful sitting about a year after I started again) until the Master came in person and gave it back to me.

Some months later, in the Spring of 1962, I learned that there would be a big gathering of disciples from all over the East Coast in Boston on the first weekend in May. I had not seen any brothers or sisters since I had left the Path more than two years before. I wanted to go, but I was afraid. I was afraid that the others would be more spiritual than I; that they would judge and condemn me for having left the Path; that I would not be at home in such rarified company, and that I would not like it; and I was afraid of the hazards or uncertainty that precedes anything new, or any major departure from the norm. But I also wanted to go, very much.

I drove down to Boston on a beautiful Saturday morning and, since the meeting was to be held on Marlboro Street, I parked my old Jeep station wagon in a parking lot near where Marlboro Street runs into the Public Gardens. Then I walked up the street. As I grew nearer to the building where the meetings were being held, all my fears rose up in one mighty rush, and I began to sweat and tremble. The closer I came, the more certain I was that I couldn't go in. I was noticing the numbers on the doors and, as I drew abreast of the correct house, I made up my mind with absolute conviction: "No! I will *not* go in: I'll call up some of my old buddies and drink beer with them." And I kept on walking.

Not more than three steps later, a large, heavy-set white-haired woman, neatly dressed in black, whom I had never seen before, stood squarely in my way and spoke to me: "Hey! Do you know which house this Hindu thing is in?" I said politely, "I believe it's in that one there"—pointing. She looked me in the face a moment and then said, "Come on! Let's go in!" grabbed me by the wrist with a vise-like grip and led me into the house, up the stairs, right into the meeting room.

Now this woman was a real person; I later got to know her a little bit, although we never discussed this incident. She was a real person, not an apparition conjured up by the Master. But if she had been an apparition, the effect of her appearance on me could not have been greater. This was the second time that the Master had deliberately and directly interceded with me to save me from myself and, while it would not be the last time, in some respects it remains in my memory as the most miraculous of all my experiences with him. This incident, in bright sunlight on Marlboro Street in Boston, with the Master working through the form of an old fat woman, perhaps symbolizes better than any other the basic benevolence of the Universe, once an individual seeker has committed himself to its care. For the fact is that those two days of meetings were wonderful; no one judged me; I was treated with great love and respect by everyone; all my fears proved groundless, and I received an enormous lift. Had I not gone in I doubt that I would have survived. I needed very badly the company of those who were doing the same thing I was. I had gone as far as I could alone, and the Master knew it.

A few months later the Master's American Representative asked me to hold Satsang in Sanbornton. I was reluctant to do so, and wrote the Master myself to make sure it was really all right with him. He replied that he was glad to learn that I was holding Satsang! My reluctance continued, however, and it was another six months before I started doing it.

That September (1962) we purchased the abandoned farm that later became known as "Sant Bani Ashram." It was never, at any time, our intention to found an ashram. We were looking for an isolated place in the country to live quietly and raise our kids. We named our place "Sant Bani Farm" (I took the name from an old book published during Baba Sawan Singh's lifetime by the "Sant Bani Book Depot"; the name stuck with me—it has various meanings in Sanskrit and Hindi: "The Teachings of the Saints," "The Voice of the Saints," etc.) and I felt moved to name our farm accordingly, although it did not seem particularly appropriate.

In December 1962 occurred my last encounter with an esoteric school other than Sant Mat. Some friends of ours, also initiated, had left the Path and were studying with Willem Nyland, a teacher of the Gurdjieff system who had known and studied with Gurdjieff personally. Because *In Search of the Miraculous* had played such an important part in my own search, and because it was really getting difficult for me to practice the Path in the continuing physical absence of my Guru, I was intensely curious, and we attended the meetings with Mr. Nyland for about a month. I was greatly impressed by him—he seemed the freest man I had met up to that point—and I found what he had to say really helpful. Nevertheless, every attempt on my part to put the system into practice in my life ended disastrously and I was forced to the conclusion that it was not for me: I had my Guru, my Path was laid out for me, and anything else that I did was only an evasion of the work that I had to do. It seemed clear to me, though, that Gurdjieff's teaching and Kirpal Singh's teaching sprang ultimately from the same source, as there were many points of contact: the psychology of both systems especially were similar. I understood this better later on when the writings of Idries Shah proved conclusively that Gurdjieff's system was derived from the Sufis. Since Sant Mat was taught by many Sufi Masters (including the grestest of all, Jal-al-luddin Rumi, as well as Rabia Basri, Shamas Tabrez, Bulleh Shah, Hazrat Bahu, and many others) it was evident that the chances of contact were great.

Shortly after we stopped attending the Nyland meetings, we began holding Satsang (in January 1963); those meetings have continued since then without a break.

That Spring we learned that the Master might be making his second world tour very soon. Skeptical at first because we had heard similar rumors many times before, we nonetheless invited him to visit our farm. We never dreamed that he would really come: attendance at our weekly meetings was still tiny, and there was only one person besides ourselves who had taken the initiation. But to our intense amazement and joy, and against all consistencies of logic, he accepted our invitation.

In June we learned that he had left India and was actually

in Europe, on the first leg of his tour. Sometime in August we received a copy of the tour schedule and found that he would arrive in Washington, D.C., on the first of September, and that he would be at Sant Bani Farm on October 11. Incredible! Five years after our initiation, and two years after we had come back to the Path, we were going to see our Master in the flesh.

2. America 1963-64

He did arrive in the United States on September 1, 1963, a Sunday, and although we missed the first sight of him at the airport, we saw him later that same day. I think everyone can imagine the excitement and anticipation mixed with a little fear (suppose he wasn't what he was supposed to be?) that was with us all during the long trip from New Hampshire down to Washington. When we got there it was about 3:30 p.m., and Mr. Khanna told us that Master was just leaving for the Friends Meeting House to hold Satsang, and we could follow him over. We jumped in the car, backed into a driveway across the street so that we were facing the house directly, and just at that instant Master came out! We had a marvelous darshan for just half a minute; even now, after seeing him many hundreds of times, I cannot forget that first incredible sight of him coming out of the house and getting into the car. Just the way he held his magnificent head and walked out was moving beyond words. At sight of him, Judith burst into tears; and I was overwhelmed with a sense of my own triviality. Seeing him, I understood instantly why the books lay such stress on the company of Saints.

Master stayed in Washington for 27 days, but we were only there for three of them; our house was badly in need of a great deal of work before it would be fit for him. The

night we were due to leave, he granted us a very sweet darshan in his room, gave us *parshad,*[1] and talked lovingly
about coming to our farm. He also told us very firmly that
we should stay over and attend the meditation he was conducting the next morning. We did.

I had never attended a group meditation conducted by
the Master before, and was totally unprepared for this one
(the first of the 1963 tour). After giving us really excellent
instructions, he left the room for an hour while we sat; on
returning, he questioned each person individually as to
what he had seen. The problem was, as usual, I had seen
nothing; I hadn't expected anything different really; it
didn't bother me, because it was what I was used to. I noticed, however, with a real sense of foreboding, that out of
a hundred people or so in the room, I was one of maybe
four that hadn't seen any light at all. Person after person
reeled off their experiences while I listened incredulously;
even my wife had had an experience! But not me.

By the time Master reached me, I had irrationally worked
myself up into some kind of weird depression in which I was
blaming Master for not giving me anything. He looked at
me. "Yes?" "Nothing, sir" (sullenly). "Nothing?"
"Nothing." He fixed me with the most penetrating gaze I
had ever seen. "Why not?" "I don't know, sir." "Were
you conscious of your breathing?" "No, sir." "Did you
have a headache?" "No, sir." "Then why not?" "I don't
know, sir." (In my heart I was thinking, Aren't you supposed to know that? Isn't it your fault?) Master looked at me
again. Oh, God, that gaze! "Everyone else had this thing;
why not you?" I was defeated: I said weakly, "I don't

1. *Parshad* is any gift, but especially food, given by a Master: it carries
his charging.

know, sir." He looked at me again. "Are you initiated?" (Oh God, I thought. Oh God! Doesn't he know whether I'm initiated or not? Oh God, oh God!) "Yes, sir." "Did you have an experience when you were initiated?" "Yes, sir." "If you had then, why not now?" 'I don't know, sir." He looked at me again, a long, long look. "All right; go and sit over there; I will give you another sitting later." I did not get another sitting; we had to leave too soon. In the car on the way home, all the pent-up rage and frustration and humiliation burst through, and for many minutes I am afraid that I cursed the name of the Son of God: I can say this because I know that he has long since forgiven me.

(Later of course it became perfectly clear to me what Master had been doing with me in those minutes: He had been giving me a crash course in humility and ego-smashing which I desperately needed if there was to be any hope for me at all. He knew perfectly well, of course, exactly who I was and if I was initiated or not: just the night before he had assured me that he would come to our farm. But every one of his questions was aimed at breaking down a very hard rock of arrogance which was effectively preventing any further development. Just two nights previously I had been introduced as a group leader, much to my ego's satisfaction; to be asked by the Master himself in front of the same peo ple if I was initiated or not was so humiliating it was unbearable. But Masters don't fool around; they look into the heart of the disciple and give him what is required in order to bring about the greatest possible growth.)

Eventually I calmed down, and even the nightmare of those minutes faded away; remaining were the very moving recollections of the way Master looked as he moved about, the loving darshan that he had given us, and the sense of timelessness that had pervaded the whole stay; as though we had stepped out of the modern world for a few days. Anyway, we had a great deal of work to do, preparing for his visit; so much work that there was literally no time for morbidity. We worked day and night; I had left my job and Judith and I did nothing but work on the house twelve or fourteen hours a day. My meditations which were no good anyway were forgotten about (Judith kept hers up by getting by with two hours sleep a night—literally); all sense of a future was lost—as far as we were concerned, the world ended on October 11 (the day Master was coming). Those were difficult days in many ways, but I think they were the happiest days of my life up to that point, despite the fact that the repairs on the house involved our going into debt with absolutely no assurance of being able to pay it back. But we could see only one thing—the Master was coming!

The next time we saw him was in Boston at Mildred Prendergast's house where he was staying.

He was sitting on Millie's bed, crosslegged. His face seemed sad, and the total effect of his presence was that he seemed too large for the room. He looked at me and asked right away, "How are your meditations?" (Oh, no!) "Not so good." "Why not?" I started to say, "Because I've been working on the house, getting ready for you," but didn't. Somehow, something in me knew better. He looked at me. "Are you initiated?" This time half of my mind gave up and spun off a great distance away. From what seemed like many miles I heard my voice say, "Yes, Master." "When were you initiated?" "May 1958, Master." He looked thoughtful. "Five years. That's a long time." Suddenly I realized that while his words were hard, his tone was very gentle; and I saw the love in His gaze. He asked me very softly, "What is the use of taking the Initiation if you are not going to do anything with it?" Suddenly the part of my mind that was away came back, and I felt with that question, It's going to be all right. I looked at him. "No use, Master." But I was beginning to understand.

That night Master gave the second of three discourses at the Second Church in Boston. It was difficult to follow his talk: the accoustics were bad and there was a decided echo; but if ever a Biblical prophet stood in a Christian church it was that night.

Two days later, on Thursday, October 10 (his last day in Boston, and the day before he came to Sant Bani) he gave Initiation. Something very strong told me to attend that Initiation, and I did. I got up early on a frosty morning and drove down to Boston, my heart singing; Master had given me peace, though I could see no reason for it. At the Initiation, the first ever that I had attended with Master personally conducting, he gave me back everything I had lost and more besides. Never in my life had I swum in the Ocean of Light as I did that blessed golden morning in Boston. "Oh God, thank you, Oh God, thank you," I kept saying over and over, tears in my eyes. After the sitting the Master came around asking the new initiates what they had seen. He came to the back where we older ones were sitting and asked cheerfully, "Everything all right here?" I could say nothing; I looked at him and caught his eye, and he twinkled. Oh thank God! Thank God! And it was all him; he knew all about everything and always had!

The following day he came to Sant Bani Farm, and our new life in him began. Later it seemed that the great gulf fixed between the old and the new opened on this day. One twenty-four hour period and what changes it wrought! All of the hard work and the nightmare anxiety of the previous five weeks faded away in the unearthly joy those twenty-four hours brought. After it was over, I reflected that it was the one event in my life that had not only been as good as I could have imagined, but infinitely better. I understood for the first time what it is like to be loved—really loved—by Someone Who knew what I really was. I had a taste, that is, of the love of God.

I had gone (with our three-and-a-half-year old daughter Miriam) to the nearest exit off Interstate 93 to meet him and the caravan (five or six cars) that was accompanying him. When we arrived at Sant Bani, I jumped out of my car and rushed over to his. Judith, with our two-year old son, Eric, in her arms was already greeting him. He spoke to us very kindly, and slowly climbed the little hill on which the house stood. When he reached the front door, he turned and looked slowly and thoughtfully over the beautiful New Hampshire landscape spread out before him. He laughed and said, very quietly, almost under his breath, "Nature is always beautiful, except when tormented by man." Then he went in the house.

A little later Judith and I were looking out the back window when we saw him walking up the little hill behind the house to a large and prominent rock under a cherry tree. He was accompanied only by Bibi Hardevi (called Tai Ji), his housekeeper who looked after his needs. When he reached the rock, he took off his turban and lay down on the grass, Tai Ji squatting nearby. Judith and I watched wide-eyed; we nudged each other in suppressed excitement. What happened then was surely the most light-hearted Satsang ever! As the disciples discovered where he was, they gathered around him (there were about fifteen or twenty people) while he sat on the rock, put them in meditation, tossed them *parshad* apples, joked and teased with them, took pictures of them (because they had been taking pictures of him) and in general made them very happy. But not me: I and three others were at the Unitarian Church in nearby Franklin, where the Master was scheduled to speak that night, getting the auditorium ready for his talk. We missed the whole thing.

That night the Master gave his talk, and a very good talk it was, to a good-sized crowd which asked interesting questions afterward.

Toward the end of the talk, he mentioned that he was happy to have spent the day at "Sant Bani Ashram." This was the first time that our farm had ever been referred to in that way, and our subsequent use of the term dates from that moment.

Judith rode to the church that night in the car with the Master. On the way in, he said to her, "Your husband missed everything this afternoon." She explained, and he nodded.

The following morning a group meditation was held at our now-ashram. It was the first time I had meditated since the Master had given me back the light two days before. This time the Light was even more intense and more bright; and through it I caught glimpses of much more. When the Master came to me afterward, I told him what I had seen, and he twinkled. Later I went up to him and said, "I just want to thank you for that beautiful meditation this morning. I know I couldn't have done it by myself." He looked at me and said, matter-of-factly, "Well, you missed all the fun yesterday," and smiled into my eyes.

Later that same morning he was standing behind the big house alone, and I went up to him: "Last night I heard you refer to this place as an ashram. Judith and I have talked it over, and we agreed that we would like to give it to you." He said, "You keep custody! Maintain it according to my teachings, that's all."

We all left around noontime, after an orgy of picture-taking, for Kirpal Ashram in Vermont, managed by Nina Gitana. That night the Master spoke at Goddard College in nearby Plainfield. I was standing in the back of the hall, watching him intently; I was amazed to see that all through the talk his face kept literally changing into that of his Master, Baba Sawan Singh of Beas, who died in 1948. I had often heard of this phenomenon but had never before personally witnessed it, although I was to see it fairly often from this time on. It was a very specific and tangible thing: he would look down a moment, in the course of his talk, and when he lifted his head again, he would *be* Sawan Singh completely. Throughout the talk his features kept shifting back and forth in this way.

The next few weeks are a kaleidoscope of memories: an evening in Jackson, New Hampshire, with the Master standing in the middle of a circle of Sant Bani area people and talking to us like old friends; the way from Vermont to Hampton, New Hampshire, when I was supposedly leading the way in my old green GMC pickup truck (because of my alleged knowledge of New England) and managed to make the wrong turn, thus dragging the Master and all his party miles out of the way; on the same trip, the Howard Johnson's (now defunct) at Boscawen, New Hampshire, where, while the party was eating, the Master was pacing alone at the far end of the parking lot, and I went up to him and apologized for having lost the way and inconvenienced him; his total and utter lack of comprehension of what I was talking about, until, after a many-seconds blank stare, a magnificent smile burst over his face, and he said, with consummate forgiveness, "Oh, *that's* all right" (a small incident, no doubt, but terribly important to me, and a symbol of what "forgive and forget" means); driving my pickup full of the party's luggage and traveling equipment through Connecticut, coming to the Merritt Parkway where trucks are not allowed, and discovering that the Master did not wish to drive on the Parkway if I and my truck couldn't go on it; my being moved almost to tears at this and driving the truck away very fast so that the Master would have to go on the Parkway, as I couldn't bear the thought of delaying him again; arriving in Toronto late at night, with Judith and the others, almost penniless, and having Master greet us so warmly, again as if we were old friends; the radiantly beautiful wedding in Toronto, when the bright movie lights illuminated his incredible face so that every line seemed etched in acid; the motel in Louisville, when the Master stuck his head in the window of our Corvair sedan, saw the mattress we had in lieu of our back seat (so that the children could play or sleep, as they wished) and chuckled about our traveling home.

In Louisville we said goodbye to him for what we were sure was the last time, because our money (including a borrowed $500) had finally run out and the future looked bleak. That afternoon I had a private interview with him; he was sitting cross-legged and his smile was dazzling. "Well," he said first thing, "When are you going back to that very sweet place?" I told him we were leaving early the next morning. He nodded and asked me if I needed any money. I was taken by surprise; I did, of course, but the thought of taking money from my Master did not appeal to me and I said "No." (This was the first time the Master had offered me money, but was not to be the last; eventually I learned how to respond more appropriately.)

That night the Master was leaving Louisville for Minneapolis by train. I went to the station to see him off—the last time, for all I knew, that I might ever see him. In prospect, I had felt sad—these weeks with Him had been the happiest I had ever known. But when we were actually at the station, standing on the steps of the train seconds before it pulled away, I felt such intense happiness at being with Him again that all I could do was laugh. The joy of being with Him in the present was stronger than the sorrow of leaving Him in the future.

At other times, when I left Him, the sorrow would take over after the parting had happened; this time, the joy remained and settled into a sort of blissful calm. Maybe something in me knew that I was going to see him again, and in a very short time too. Whether I knew it or not, that is exactly what happened: Judith's parents chose that time to make over to her some money they had been holding for her in trust, and just three weeks after the farewell in Louisville, we were on our way to California, our debts paid and our hopes high—we planned to stay with him for the rest of the tour, if he didn't mind.

Three days before we left, President Kennedy was assassinated. My insurance man told me while I was paying up for the coming year. I couldn't believe it—I stumbled out to the car to discover that Judith had been told simultaneously by a passer-by. We were both stunned—I had once pushed John Kennedy in a wheelchair back and forth between his room and the X-ray department for the better part of a day when I had been a hospital orderly. He had impressed me very much, and I wanted him for President almost before he did. I thought he was a wonderful President, and while I am no expert on the ins and outs of national Karma, I felt and still feel that if he had lived, not only would he be remembered as one of our greatest Presidents, but that the terrible wrenching traumas of the Johnson-Nixon years would never have happened. I later learned that the Master had deep respect and appreciation for Kennedy's—indeed, all the Kennedys'—efforts.

We—Judith, Miriam, Eric and I—left for Santa Barbara, California, the day after Thanksgiving 1963. We drove almost non-stop, spending one night in Amarillo, Texas. Somewhere in Arizona the strain grew intolerable and Judith and I had a terrible fight. I mention this only because of its possible bearing on what happened next.

We reached Santa Barbara just four and a half days after leaving New Hampshire, and about an hour before the Master arrived from San Jose. When we finally saw him, he seemed very glad to see us. There was a reception scheduled for him that night in the home where he was to be staying, and all the local satsangis, as well as those who were following him from other places, attended. We for our parts were so happy to see him again that we just sat at his feet and drank deep—a long, beautiful, loving reunion. After some time, when it became evident that we were the only ones paying attention to him—at this party that was given for him— he ordered us to go mingle with the others. We were grateful for what we had been given however—especially in light of what was about to happen.

The next morning, after the meditation, the Master came up to me and said, smiling, "Well, Russell—how long are you going to stay with me?" A flash of fear went over me: I thought, if I tell him the truth—that we want to stay for the rest of the tour—maybe he won't like it! So I answered evasively, "Oh—a while, Master." His eyes narrowed: he looked at me closely: "A while? How long is a while?" "Oh—just a while, Master." He turned and walked away; and that was the last time he looked at me or spoke to me lovingly for two weeks.

The following day he was sitting at a little table on the

patio behind the house he was staying in, again just after morning meditation; he had been giving interviews, but they had just ended, and a member of his party humorously took me by the hand and led me up to the Master, saying, "Come on, Russell Perkins, you have an interview too!" I was certainly willing and I marched right up to him, bright and eager to talk with him, but the closer I got the less eager I was—because *he was not there*. His eyes were looking at me, but he was not seeing me. I stood silently for a few minutes, then, feeling vaguely ashamed, sneaked away. This was the moment that I realized that something was terribly wrong, although I did not connect it with my evasiveness and dishonesty toward Him until much later.

The only saving grace during this time was the growing relationship between my daughter Miriam and the Master. When she had first met him at Sant Bani Ashram, she had been shy; there is a picture, taken there, of her turning away from him and refusing an apple he is trying to give her. But that shyness didn't last long, and during the stay in California she became very determined to be with him as much as possible. If we couldn't find her, we would go directly to the Master's room; there she would be, standing near the door, out of the way, looking up at Him while He wrote letters or talked with visitors or whatever He was doing. We would remove her with apologies but the Master would wave his hand and say that she was no trouble, that he liked her there.

The Master spoke one Sunday morning at the Unity Church of the Valley in La Crescenta. After the service was over, as we were in the parking lot preparing to go, he came up to us and addressed Miriam: "Who do you love more—me or her?" pointing to Judith. A hard question for a three-and-a-half-year old! Miriam clung to her mother. The

Master looked at her, his eyes twinkling and kind, his voice insistent: "Who do you want to ride back with—them or me?" Suddenly shy again, she said nothing. I whispered to her, "Don't you want to ride in Master's car?" She shook her head. The Master smiled, said "All right," and left us. As soon as we were in our car, ready to follow Him out, Miriam erupted with a terrifying, blood-curdling scream: "Daddy! Hurry up! Stay close! Don't lose him!" and then began to sob uncontrollably. All the way back I struggled to keep his car in view; all the way back Miriam cried as though she were coming apart inside.

Another incident, this time in Tustin: the Master was staying in a house at the top of a very high hill, almost a mountain. The parking lot was separated from the house by a great gulf forested which led into a grassy valley accessible from both the house and the parking lot. On one occasion, after we had parked, the four of us stood for a moment looking down into the grassy valley, when suddenly we saw the Master all alone, walking purposefully down into the valley straight to a tree, where he sat down and removed his turban. Delighted, we watched him until suddenly we saw a little figure headed down into the valley from our side, going straight to him. It was Miriam, and we hadn't even noticed she had left us. She went to him and sat down beside him. There were just the two of them. We did not disturb.

Later I asked a friend of mine who had joined them later if she had any idea of what had gone on between them. She said only that when she got there they were engrossed in conversation, and that Master had said to her, "She is my friend." Miriam herself would not tell us, and now she cannot: she has forgotten. Although she is not actively practicing the Path, the Master remained personally very interested in her welfare; that she is very dear to him, and is under his protection and care, is a source of gratitude on my part.

Apart from these flickers of light, however, these weeks are among the darkest in my memory. For the intimate loving relationship I thought I had established with him was over, and the Master seemed not to care whether I was there or not. Day after day went by, and he totally ignored me: he did not glance into my eyes or speak to me, even when I was standing in a place where it was difficult for him not to. I felt that I didn't exist, that I was a cipher, nothing. This combined with the strain of following him with the whole family made me desperate. I began to rack my brains: Why is he treating me this way? Why? Why? What have I done? Since I could not or would not (at this point) face up to my evasiveness and dishonesty in Santa Barbara, I lunged here and there at any possible explanation I could dredge up. The obvious conclusion was that I wasn't meant to be with him. Once I had thought of that, I was tortured with guilt over not earning my own living. I felt like a parasite.

Judith did not share my feelings, and she did not want to leave the Master—not at all. Since my thoughts were driving me to one conclusion—I should go—and since she refused to go, I realized that leaving the Master meant leaving my wife. I did not mind this: the strain had been so great, and the feeling of everything turning bad and sour was so pervading, that I was happy to leave everything behind and start again.

I asked for an interview the last afternoon in Tustin, thinking that maybe he would clear everything up. But he did not. I asked him if he would rather I weren't with him, and he said impatiently, "Dear friend, that is up to you. *I* don't mind. If you can afford it . . ." His attitude throughout was stern and distant and I left him surer than ever that I would have to leave.

The next morning the Master and everyone left for Beaumont, California, not far from Palm Springs, in the desert. We drove there too, but somehow got our signals crossed and managed to reach everywhere the Master had gone sometime after he had left. That evening I told Judith that I could stand it no longer, and asked her to drive me to the bus station. I told her she could write me care of General Delivery, San Francisco, kissed her and the kids goodbye and got on the bus for Los Angeles, where I took the bus to San Francisco.

It is important to clarify here that even though I was leaving the Master physically, I had not stopped believing in him. On the contrary: I had become convinced that he didn't want me around, and to that extent I was still trying to please him. There was more to it than that, of course: even though I still saw what he was, and recognized him as the Master, I had lost the *connection* between him and me, and I felt now that, regardless of his greatness or the truth of the Path, *I couldn't do it*. It was too much for me. So as I rode through the California night my dominant feeling was relief. The strain that I had been living under was broken.

When I arrived in San Francisco, I took a motel room and debated what to do next. My mind, which had been a whirlpool, now became a cesspool: storms of insatiable sexuality and unrestrained violence raged over it. For three days I was jerked this way and that by the terrible power of my own thoughts. But I had no regrets about leaving, and I felt that it was inevitable. I missed my kids, but my only other emotion was continued relief that I had escaped.

After three days (approximately) I made my decision: I would go to Seattle, where my sister lived, and start a new life there. Making that decision gave me some peace, and I went to the airline office downtown to buy my ticket. As I left the office, I thought, "I had better check at the post office to see if a letter from Judith is there. I would love to hear about the kids." I was handed a letter with Judith's familiar handwriting on the envelope, and I opened it up and started reading. I had read several sentences before I realized that it was not a letter from Judith at all—it was a letter from the Master! This is what it said.

Dear Russell—

I was shocked to learn how you left for San Francisco without seeing me—I have so much love for you, and have great appreciation of the sacrifice of you both that you are making by leaving your hearth and home and accompanying me throughout—I was wondering if you may not be undergoing any financial stringency—I have love for you and you are on my mind—Be rest assured I would love you to be with me—if otherwise not inconvenient for you.

With all love,

Yours affectionately,
KIRPAL SINGH

When I finished reading it the first time, I thought, "Well this is really a very nice letter from the Master; I will have to write and thank him for it, but I can't go back"—then I read it again—and again—and again—and I went back to the airline office as fast as I could and I changed my ticket from Seattle to Houston: I could not get back to him fast enough. Somehow that letter changed everything. The nightmare was over; I knew that whatever had been wrong had been righted. In my personal affairs also: I suddenly missed Judith terribly and longed to see her again. It was as though a great fountain of forgiving love had erupted out of that humble handwritten note and cascaded over me washing away all the hurt and fear and despair and making everything right.

I arrived in Houston the night before the Master did, and the next morning I was waiting for him when he arrived. He took one look at me and smiled: a loving warm smile, and I knew that everything really was all right. I thanked him for his beautiful letter, and he said, "Your family is all right; they will be here soon." I said, "I hope so, Master," and he replied, "I am telling you that it's true: they are all right and they will be here soon." And within half an hour, it happened: Judith and the kids were there, and I felt like I had come back home and it was so good.

Judith filled me in on some of the things that had happened while I was gone. After driving me to the bus she had gone straight to Master and told him what had happened. He had said. "All right, you write him a letter and I will write him a letter." Then he had written out his letter right then, and given it to Judith. She did not, however, write a letter of her own, but had simply addressed the envelope and mailed it with the Master's letter in it.

I discovered also that she had had a very hard time without me. The Master had flown from Los Angeles to Dallas, which meant that those who were driving had to drive non-stop if they were going to see him at all. In my absence, Judith had no one to share the driving with, and she had to drive all day and night without sleep while taking care of the small children. It was really a heroic feat. At one point she fell asleep at the wheel, the car went off the road and nearly turned over; the kids were thrown from one side to the other, but Judith, waking up at the last minute, did very intense Simran and the kids didn't even wake up, let alone get hurt.

It was difficult for her in other ways too. She told me that when she finally reached Dallas, exhausted, she left the kids in the car while she went into a restaurant (with others who were following the Master). Coming out from the restaurant, she was dismayed to see, at a table near the door, Miriam and Eric, our kids, in the company of a policeman. When she claimed them, the policeman told her that it was against the law in Dallas to leave children in a parked car, and lectured her blisteringly on what an irresponsible mother she was.

Also in Dallas, the other followers (some of them) began to complain that Miriam and Eric were dirtier than they ought to be. Judith was at her wits' end trying to be herself and me at the same time—what could she do? Once the Master stopped at her table while she was eating and said compassionately, "Your children are disheveled. In this country, that's a crime." All in all, my sudden departure had caused more than its share of difficulty and suffering for her, and we were both ecstatically happy to be reunited.

The following day the Master was scheduled to visit a prospective ashram site some distance from Houston. Judith had taken the children and gone to the laundromat, hoping to get a wash done before everyone left. But before she got back, the Master was out on the sidewalk, ready to go. I had been waiting there, just hoping to see him, and I was enjoying his presence again. He waited and waited, but no car came. Finally he turned to me and said with a big smile, "Car of Burt?" I knew instantly what he meant—a disciple had donated a car that was available for whatever use the Master wanted to put it to. Although in most places, there was some local disciple who wanted to drive him, still this other car was always there. I said, "You want me to get it for you and drive you, Master?" Smiling, he said, "Yes." I was beside myself with joy—to drive the Master was a long-held desire of mine that had never yet been fulfilled. I raced over to the parking lot and found another disciple just getting into it. I jumped in ahead of him, took the keys out of his hand, shouted, "The Master told me to get it!" and drove off, leaving him standing there.

When I drove around on to the street, I saw the Master was talking to someone. I pulled up beside him, and he got in and sat down, while continuing to talk with whoever it was, so that his back was turned away from me. I was looking at him anyway when I heard a voice from outside my window say, "Get out, Russell!" I whirled my head around. It was the owner of the car, his face grim. I stared. He replied, "Get out, Russell. You're not going to drive this car. I am." I couldn't believe it. I said, "But Master told me to"—He said, "That's all right. He didn't know. Now get out!" *Master didn't know!* What was going on?[2] I looked over at him, but he was still absorbed in the conversation; so, almost ready to cry, my joy curdled into bitter disappointment, I climbed heavily out of the driver's seat and walked around to Master's side. Master looked up and saw me. His eyes opened wide and he said, "What—?" and turned instantly around and looked at the new driver, who said placatingly, "That's all right, Master. I'm going to drive." Instantly comprehending the wholeness of the situation, he turned back to me and said, eyes twinkling, "Would you like to ride next to me?" and patted the seat between him and the driver with his left hand.

Now this was a very great honor: it was rare for anybody to ride in the front seat with him, let alone me. But my traumatic disappointment over not driving him had forced a sudden change of perspective, and I was now acutely aware that Judith and the children had not yet returned,

---

2. The owner was of course angry, and with excellent reason, over my irresponsible disappearance, and was invoking his property rights accordingly. Several years later he apologized to me for this incident.

and I was feeling responsible for them: if I went off now with Master, how would they know where to go? I had put her through too much in the last few days to inflict this upon her now.

So I said, with a brave smile, "That's all right, Master; my wife isn't back yet, and I think I'd better wait for her—" Someone in the back seat interrupted me: "To hell with the wife! The Master invited you, you should go. It's a great honor, you see!" But Master silenced him and smiled at me so lovingly, and said, "All right; wait for your wife," and I felt in my heart that he was not displeased.

I tried to find out from the others where exactly they were going, but I couldn't. It was as though there was a conspiracy, although I don't really think there was. Nevertheless, all I could learn was that they were going down some highway and the general direction (both of which I have long since forgotten). Before I could find out any more than that, they had all climbed in their cars and driven away; the last car to go was Leon Poncet's distinctive blue van. Then I was standing alone on the sidewalk, watching them disappear around the corner. My eyes began to mist and my mouth to tremble as I walked into the hotel. Then all the ups and downs of the last few days, and especially the heartbreakingly overwhelming ache at being once again separated from my Master, so soon after rediscovering Him, pressed down on my heart and I began to cry as I had never cried in my life: it was as though there was a thunderstorm going on inside me, giving vent to a never-ending torrent of tears.

When Judith came in maybe twenty minutes later, she found me lying across the bed, still crying. She tried and tried to find out what was wrong, but I wouldn't tell her: I just kept on crying. Finally after many minutes had passed, she got me to sit up and calm down, and I told her everything that had happened that morning, including the departure of the Master and everyone else to the proposed ashram site almost an hour before. She was thoughtful. Then she said, "Come on! Let's go too!" I started crying again: "But how? I don't know where to go!" She said, calmly, "We know they went on the highway, and we know which direction. What have we got to lose? Come on!" Without any hope, I agreed that we had nothing to lose and we set out.

We had been on the highway not more than ten minutes when I saw a long line of cars obviously traveling together up ahead. I couldn't believe that this was the Master's caravan; after all, they had had a head start of more than an hour. Yet the last car bore a vivid resemblance to Leon Poncet's blue van. I picked up speed, my heart pounding: Yes, by God, by the living breathing six-foot tall God Who played with time and space as if they were His own personal toys, it was the same caravan that had left Houston more than an hour before, driving along the turnpike as though nothing at all were amiss. Smiling gratefully, with a prayer of joy in my heart, I drove up behind the caravan and quietly joined it; neither Judith nor I said much, but we both quietly enjoyed our own personal miracle, and we have never forgotten it, nor will we ever forget it.

That night the Master spoke at a Trade Center; I was in the audience, and for the second time in my life I observed him changing into Baba Sawan Singh. This time the room was brilliantly lit, and it would perhaps be more correct to say that Baba Sawan Singh gave the talk and occasionally changed into Kirpal Singh. Several others, to my personal knowledge, also observed this and commented on it to me afterward.

The next day was Christmas. That night the Master spoke at St. James Episcopal Church and the talk he gave on the mystery of Christ became well known: it was later published under the title "God Power, Christ Power, Guru Power," has gone through many printings, and is included in the Master's book of short writings, *The Way of the Saints.* I however did not attend that talk, as it was my turn to watch the kids. Soon after everyone got back from the talk (but not Judith who was late), I got a phone call to come up to the Master's room: he was having a party. I looked at the kids: they were sound asleep, our room was just around the corner from the desk on the first floor, and I took a chance that they would be all right. I went up. The Master was very pleased to see me. He was sitting on a couch, his feet on the floor, a coffee table in front of him. On the coffee table was a big bowl full of gigantic nuts, still in their shells, which he was giving out for parshad.

When he saw me he said joyously. "How many children you have got?" I said, "Two, Master," although I knew he knew well how many there were. He said, laughing, "You will be the gainer," as he poured nuts into my waiting hands until they cascaded on to my lap and down to the floor. "For you and your children," he explained. Then, when he saw my happy happy face looking up at him, he said softly, "I liked your place the best—and you left me." I felt as though I had been stabbed, but he continued to joke with me and kept me near him. Judith came in at some point and also got an overload of parshad, then Bibi Hardevi began talking in Hindi. The Master laughed and requested a member of his party to translate. This is what she was saying: When Master sat on the rock under the tree at Sant Bani Ashram, Guru Nanak[3] had appeared to him and told him

3. A famous sixteenth-century Saint, in the direct line of Kirpal Singh.

that he also used to rest in just the same way on his travels. Tai Ji could hear the Master talking but she could not see Guru Nanak. She became indignant and requested Master to make it possible for her to see Guru Nanak also, which he did. Then she was happy.

At one of the Houston Satsangs I was outside watching the Children (Judith and I used to take turns attending the meetings) and I had, as was my habit after the children had gone to sleep in the car, crept into the back of the hall for just a few seconds—just enough to have a look at him. (I used to go back and forth quite a lot between the hall and the car.) On the night I am remembering, as I was standing just outside the outside door, it opened and a couple came out accompanied by a member of the Master's party. They were arguing. When he saw me, he said to the couple, "Talk to him—he left everything for the Master's sake," and disappeared back into the hall. I looked at the couple. The man was angry and the woman was embarrassed. I asked them what was wrong. The man said, "Why can't he talk so we can understand him?" I was incredulous: "What?" "Why can't he talk so we can understand him? What is the use of his making this trip and giving talks if we can't understand a word he says?" A wave of anger began to rise somewhere in my stomach. I said, "You can't be serious! I can understand him perfectly." He said, "I'm very serious. Have you ever read Yogananda's *Autobiography*?" Of course I had. "Do you remember how he couldn't speak English, and then on the ship when he had to give a talk, he just opened his mouth and English came out?" The unfairness of his attitude grated on me, and I said, heatedly, "That's not a fair comparison! Yogananda

His life story is told in *Servants of God* by Jon Engle (Sanbornton: Sant Bani Ashram, 1980).

was talking about learning English, not speaking it without an accent! I bet he had a heavy accent! And this is the first place we've been where people have complained about this. In New Hampshire he addressed an audience of brand-new people, and they asked him lots of questions afterward which showed they had understood him—the questions didn't make any sense otherwise.'' (Master's accent was fairly heavy, but his English was excellent, and it is true that most people, with a little empathy and patience, could at this stage of his life follow him fairly easily. As he grew older he became more difficult to understand.) I added ''Maybe it's your Southern accent that's causing the trouble. Why blame him?'' He looked at me and said, ''Is this part of his teaching—getting angry like this?'' I looked away—ashamed but still angry—''No. I'm sorry''—but I wasn't. I felt that Master had been stupidly, trivially, dealt with, and I was furious. Just then someone came up and said, ''The Master is giving private interviews now if you would like to see him.'' The man said, ''Yes, we would!'' and to me, ''I'm going to bring this up to him and we'll see what he says!'' and they left.

I felt sick at heart: They were going to complain to the Master about his own speech! And what had I done to help matters? I had only made him look worse by reacting in a juvenile way. Thoroughly miserable, I hung around until the couple came out. Seeing me, the man came up to me triumphantly, and said, ''I told him the same thing I said to you, and do you know what *he* said?'' I shook my head. He said, ''He looked down and said, 'Yes, I know, I have a bad speech problem!' '' I made no reply. I walked away. But Master's humility took on a new dimension for me that night, and I appreciated his greatness more than ever.

Soon he flew to Florida. We were driving: two cars (ours

and one other) were going to drive nonstop and we each agreed to look out for the welfare of the other. First we went to the airport to see him off. Just before he boarded the plane, he said to me, "Well, Russell! Are you going to leave me again?" He was looking at me with so much love I could hardly believe it. I looked up into his eyes and I felt full of love from head to toe as I said from my heart, "I will never leave You again." And I never did.

In Florida, he visited St. Petersburg and later Miami, and those stays (especially Miami) were happy times; in Miami we stayed at the home of Judith's aunt, and this made things much easier for us. Several incidents from this period stand vividly in my memory—but I no longer recall their exact chronology.

The first few days of the Master's stay in Miami, there were no public talks scheduled; all of the Satsangs were held in the home where he was staying. One night it was my turn to attend, and I was shocked at the sound of the Master's voice: it was so hoarse that it sounded like it was stretched on a rack, and he coughed—great racking coughs—constantly. The pain that he felt was so intensely real to all of us that we were sitting on needles throughout the talk. For he insisted on giving his complete talk and, except for the sound of his voice and the coughing, gave no indication at all that there was anything wrong: he was animated, a beautiful winning smile on his face, and gave a breathtakingly beautiful talk. Watching him do what he had to do that night, observing both his pain and his ability to not let it deter him, some inkling of what the crucifixion meant in real human terms seeped in; I also realized that night for the first time that the Master was going to die.

At the conclusion of the talk, after we had sighed with relief that his ordeal was at last over, he asked if there were any questions. A woman who was seeing the Master for the first time raised her hand. A member of his party jumped on her: "Why are you asking questions? Can't you see the Master is sick?" She was abashed. But the Master silenced his follower with a wave of his hand, and leaning forward, his beautiful eyes alight with love and deep concern, he said in a voice barely usable but still somehow touched with gentle compassion: "Please ask your question. Please ask it. Please?" and she did. The Master answered it completely, asked if there were more questions, and when there weren't, left the room. The next day there was no trace of his illness. Later an initiate who had been there that night told me that she had been troubled all her life with a severe throat problem, including a hacking cough; that she had aggravated the problem by smoking heavily, but while she had made many attempts to stop smoking, had been unable to do so; that she had had an interview with the Master that afternoon and told him all this, and he had told her not to worry; and that night, as he was talking and suffering, she had felt her own trouble recede; and she was able to stop smoking that night, and had never experienced her cough or throat problem again.

Shortly after this, I was standing on the lawn near the Perrins' home (where Master was staying) one afternoon when Master came up to me and beckoned me to follow him. He led me a little way off from the others and started to speak to me. The expression on his face was most peculiar—he looked like a little boy— and he reached into his inside jacket pocket and pulled out his wallet, at the same time saying, "I was thinking maybe you needed some money?—" in such a human sort of embarrassed way that a great wave of love for him just surged up within me. I refused the money—"Oh no no, Master, I can't take money from you!''—which I came later to feel was a major error; I would not have refused anything else from him and if He Who is the Giver wants to give, why should the receivers refuse? I don't know of course how much he would have given me but it is a fact that when we returned home after the tour was over we had managed to spend every cent of the money that had been made available to us, and it was five months before I could get a steady job: the bleakest poverty of our married life lay ahead, and I do not think it was unconnected with that refusal.

As I said earlier, during the stay in Miami we were able to stay in the home of Judith's Aunt Robbie.[4] This was a great blessing for us, financially and psychologically. It meant that we were not around where the Master was as much as we had been, but I thought this was a good thing: I felt that the other satsangis were getting tired of us and our kids and our problems, and that if we kept a low profile for a while, so much the better. Of course we continued to attend all the meetings, sharing the babysitting as before.

One afternoon, I was standing on the steps of Miami High School where the Master was scheduled to talk in a few minutes. I saw him arrive and start up the steps, way on the other side, accompanied by a member of his party. I was looking at him from a distance and loving him, but I did not move any nearer. Suddenly the Master veered and walked across the steps until he had reached me. He stopped in front of me and looked directly into my eyes. He was standing straight and tall and looking very stern. ''Where have

4. The widow of the philosopher John Dewey. Interestingly, Dr. Julian Johnson had mentioned Dewey, whom he had known and admired as a young man, several times in his book *The Path of the Masters*, written during the lifetime of Baba Sawan Singh. I found those passages and read them to her, and she appreciated them. She also went to hear the Master speak and loved him.

you been?'' I was completely taken aback: "Well, I—we've been staying at Judith's aunt's''—he took one step closer, said deliberately, "You should be around more. I missed you!'', raised his hand and, to my utter amazement, struck me on the chest; then without another word, turned around and walked into the building. The blow didn't hurt a bit; rather it felt warm and good, but the whole incident was and is incomprehensible to me.

After Miami, the Master left for Panama and we left for home. We drove to New Hampshire non-stop and visited our home (now Sant Bani Ashram) for the first time since November. Approximately ten days later as previously arranged, another disciple called to tell us that the Master would be returning to Washington the following day. Leaving our children with my parents, we drove to Washington immediately. The following day, January 18, 1964, a cold Saturday with an unusual (for Washington) amount of snow on the ground, the Master flew in to Friendship Airport. I was with a small group of disciples that met him there; he greeted us lovingly, happily and warmly, and was driven directly to the house of T.S. Khanna, then his American representative, who had accompanied him throughout. When we arrived at the house, he sat down in a big chair in the living room and began to talk with us, laughing and joking and prophesying, about any and all subjects. We were all *very* happy to see him again.

It is difficult to write about the ten days that followed, because for those of us fortunate to be there they were the ultimate distillation, the final focus, of our experience with the Master to date. Everything was sharpened, clarified, made vivid; details were filled in, the incomplete was completed. Every morning a meditation sitting, every evening a Satsang; there were only about a hundred persons in all attending those meetings, so that everyone felt very close to him and had plenty of opportunity to see him privately. The Master gave no public talks, but spoke intimately and with great detail to his initiates; he had Tai Ji sing many of his own *bhajans* or holy songs, and there was a great deal of humor in his talks—easy, delicious humor that reached us with an undercurrent of astonished delight at how beautiful everything was. Yet he pulled no punches: the talks given during this period were almost brutally frank in outlining what is required from those audacious enough to seek God.

The day after he arrived, on Sunday, January 19, the Master held Satsang at the Friends Meeting House in Washington. He spoke standing up, which he rarely did, and his talk was electrifying: I had the distinct feeling throughout that the whole thing was happening on many levels at once—that the Master was simultaneously speaking on the astral, causal and spiritual planes and that His Whole Being in its completeness was speaking directly to us, as Whole Beings—demanding that we become that. It was a tremendous experience, shared by all present.

Most of the Satsangs during this period were held in Mr. Khanna's living and dining rooms, which between them were just barely big enough to accommodate a hundred people with squeezing. These Satsangs were very informal, with lots of singing and laughter, and were more often conversations than lectures. Especially memorable was the night of January 23, which gives such insight into the Master's teaching methods, his story-telling ability, and his sense of humor, that I am reproducing it here in its entirety, as transcribed from the tape:[5]

5. Because so many of the questions represent an unfolding and progression on the part of the individuals asking them, the various questioners are designated as "QA," "QB," etc.

THE MASTER: "It would be better if you were to ask questions; then we will talk on it. The general talks are routine, you see. Any particular points which you would like to have clarified, you can. Any of you?"

QA: "Sometimes it's hard to distinguish when we are meditating and something comes to us, between what is a machination of the mind and what is truly a spiritual enlightenment. For instance, when we see ourselves inside or we will see things that are of a very mundane level that we are preoccupied with every day. I will sit in meditation; sometimes I don't seem to have control over these things. I don't want control over them."

THE MASTER: "Your question is mixed up with so many things. What in particular do you want?"

QA: "I want to know how to distinguish, or are we to distinguish, when these forms come to us."

THE MASTER: "The main thing is, whatever form comes within, repeat the Five Names which are charged. Anything negative will eventually go away. Sometimes the Negative Power affects you with wrong things: then repeat the Five Names. For that purpose you have been given a safeguard against all of these things."

QB: "I asked you—I think it was in California—sometimes in meditation I have this terrific vibration which I can't seem to control. And You said not to think of the body. But sometimes it's so very strong that I have to stop meditating. I get so nervous, and I feel as if I was being electrocuted or something. What can I do to stop that?"

THE MASTER: "Just do it in the right way. If you do it in the right way and don't think of the body, there will be no trouble. If anything like that happens, leave it off, that's all. And sit in the right way.''

QB: "It's so powerful that I can't help but think of the body.''

THE MASTER: "But it's not like that every day.''

QB: "No, no, but at times. And then it rises to my throat and I feel as if I was choking.''

THE MASTER: "No, no. That is due to the wrong way of doing the practice. Prana is involved.''

QB: "But I don't do any yoga techniques anymore.''

THE MASTER: "Choking of the throat cannot come unless prana is involved. Breathing is involved. First it goes slowly, at intervals; then it chokes you. That is the wrong way of doing it.''

QB: "But I don't do anything since I was initiated by You.''

THE MASTER: "These are involved: you don't do it purposely. While you are doing the practice, sometimes breathing is unknowingly involved; then naturally that choking arises.''

QB: "But you know, I'll tell you something strange. I have had that experience mostly when I have meditated when You have been there. Now, in Vancouver in the morning meditation, I sat right next to You, and it was so terrific, I got that power so much it was terrible. I mean, it was wonderful, but it was almost terrifying. And it happens more when You're around.''

THE MASTER: "It means that when I am around, there is radiation. The soul is withdrawn in a hurry. But your thought is not altogether free of the body consciousness.

That is why breathing is involved and there is choking. And sometimes it happens out of emotions, too: emotions sometimes bring on choking.

"Look here, let us give an example in a worldly way. You are going to meet your friend whom you love: perhaps it is your father, mother, brother, or anybody. And he wishes you to come alone. And even though you are going to your friend, you take so many children and other things with you. You are going to meet him and there is no time for you to speak to him. And he will also not be able to devote his whole time to you, you see? This is a worldly way of thinking. Now you have to go to God. God is all alone. Is it not so? He has no father, no mother, no brother. So naturally He wants everybody to come to Him *all alone*. He does not want you to take anything with you: no worldly things; not even your body; not even your intellect. He says, 'You come alone.' Whatever little time you devote in this way will bear forth fruit.

"When we are sitting we are not to think of outside things, not to think of the body, not to think of the breathing, not even to think of the thinking. We should be physically still and intellectually still, too. If you do it in the right way, there will be no trouble. You see?"

QB: "But if you're intellectually still, you're repeating the Five Names?"

THE MASTER: "Those become automatic. When you think of their meaning, your intellect works. If you don't think of their meaning, after a few days they become automatic. Their charging helps. You are told not to think of the meanings, although the meanings have been given to you. You are not to visualize; you are not to think of the meaning of the Names. They will go on automatically. The charging helps. Simply look sweetly and be fully absorbed. It is a question of the seeing of the soul, of the attention. Attention is the outward expression of the soul. Just as the rays of the sun enliven and enlighten the whole world, similarly the rays of the attention (the attention is the rays of the soul) enlighten the whole body. If those rays are withdrawn, the body will be dark. When the sun sets, all rays are withdrawn and there is darkness. Similarly, the body will be darkened, and there will be no thought of the body. It is only your attention that gives you the feeling of the body. So if you do it in the right way, you will have no trouble. Errors do creep in automatically, generally. Then trouble arises."

QC: "Master, may I ask a question?"

THE MASTER: "Yes, please."

QC: "You are drawn into the Radiant Form of the Master within and you want to go higher; does the Radiant Form of the Master dissolve into the Word or *Naam* or does the Radiant Form of the Master continue and remain in the higher regions?"

THE MASTER: "In the lower planes it continues, but absorption comes at every plane. When you devote your whole attention into the Form of the Master, you sometimes become absorbed, but that continues in further stages. Absorption is better. It does become that Light. You are Light; you become one; you forget; but you are conscious all the same. It does come at every step. Ultimately it becomes One, and there is no Form when you are absorbed into *Sat Naam*. Then Sat Naam takes you to the stages where there is final absorption. Otherwise, that Form continues to work in the Radiant Form on the different planes."

QD: "Master, I'd like to know when you are coming back again."

THE MASTER: "Who, I? I will never go. [*laughs*] Why are you sending me? I won't go. Physically I have to go, one way or the other. You are also not at home all day long. Now you are not in your home: physically you are not at home, but your thought is there. Is it not so? So I have come and God willed it. I have no wishes."

QE: "Master, what plane are you in when you see the golden Light?"

THE MASTER: "That is just the beginning. But in that golden Light, the Form of the Master appears. That is not the lowest."

QE: "That is not the lowest?"

THE MASTER: "The Form generally appears in golden Light.

QE: "Is that the third plane or the fourth plane?"

THE MASTER: "It is just the beginning. The Master's Form appears only when you rise sbove *Trikuti*. Yet even before that it does manifest to show that He is with you. Sometimes when you sit in a trance, the Form comes; but generally the Form appears when you cross the big star and the moon. Before that it manifests to give consolation to the initiated that I am with you, that that Power is with you."

QF: "Master, if before one is initiated, one begins by trying to be honest with oneself, and although you may feel that so far as the rules are concerned—the diet or something—this would be no problem, but within yourself you know that you still do have doubts, would you welcome into initiation one who is quite willing to admit that there is doubt, but wants to try?"

THE MASTER: "Doubt? What sort of doubt? About the theory?"

QF: "Well. I don't know."

THE MASTER: "No, no. You must know. Clarify your doubts: in what way?"

QF: "I suppose, for the uninitiated, it's the fear of the unknown or a new experience."

THE MASTER: "No, no. My point is: first try to understand the theory. Whatever you cannot understand, let that be clarified. Then take up the way. Full conviction will arise when you see things for your own self, when you are intellectually satisfied that these are the teachings of all Masters. Take it up as an experimental measure. Then, if you get something, naturally you must be convinced. Man cannot be convinced unless he sees things for his own self, and he testifies himself."

QF: "Then, if you are not certain that you are prepared and that you have answered your questions—"

THE MASTER: "I tell you, I tell you. The man in whose heart this question of the mystery of life has entered *is* fit. It is God's grace that this question has arisen. That day is the grestest in a man's life on which the question of the mystery of life enters his heart. It cannot be stamped out unless it is solved. That this question has arisen shows that God wants to give you what you hunger for. 'There is food for the hungry and water for the thirsty.' Now, there is the question of the ethical life.

"In the old days, there was the rule that when people came to the feet of the Masters, they kept them for a long time, and when they saw that they were fully developed, *then* they gave them the initiation. It is said that one King of

Bokhara went to Kabir and lived with him for about six years. He was very obedient and dutiful. Mata Loi was serving with Kabir Sahib. She recommended the king to Kabir: 'Here's the king; he has been here with us for six years; he is very quiet, very obedient. Why don't you give him initiation?' Kabir told her that he was not yet ready. And Loi asked him, 'Well, why is that, please? He is very quiet, very obedient and in every way amicable. Why do you say that he is not fit?' Kabir said, 'All right. When he goes out of the house, hide yourself in a place where he cannot see you and throw all the refuse of the house over his head and just hear what he says.' When she threw it on him, he said, 'Had this happened in my own country, I would have taken care of this!' Then Kabir asked her, 'What did you find?' She told him that the kingship had not gone because he still said, 'Had I been in my own country I would have done this and that thing.' So then another five or six years passed by. Then Kabir said, 'Well, *now* he is ready.' Loi said, 'Well, I find no difference between the first time and now.' Kabir said, 'Now again, when he leaves the house throw all this washroom filth over his head. Then hear what he says.' When she did so he said, 'Oh God, I am even worse that that! Thank you.'

"So man must be made. Man-making is difficult; the finding of God is not difficult. Now the times have changed. They are so materialistic, who is going to stay with the Master for years and abide by what He says? There is no time to spare and sit at the feet of the Masters. Even when they have some difficulty in their meditation, people say. 'Oh, I have to go to work.' I say, 'Can't you take one or two hours' leave?'

"The times have changed in the way that those who have got hunger in their minds are taken up by the Masters. The

Masters take up the work of preparation of making a man as well as giving him the way—at the same time—and the maintenance of diaries for self-introspection from day to day is prescribed. The Masters give seekers the experience then and there, so that when they come in contact with that higher Light and Sound Principle, it will grow familiar and help them while they are at the same time weeding out all imperfections from day to day. They just say, 'Take heed that the Light which is within you is not darkened.'

"So the present times have changed, and those who have an inkling, a desire, are put on the way. They are given some experience, with the grace of God, to start with. Otherwise people are not going to believe you. 'Go on doing it, and you will have it after you do that. Do it, go on, do it. All help will be granted to you.' People have been coming to me who have been initiated somewhere. They had been putting in meditation time of two, three or four hours daily. With all that, they got nothing, and they left it. If you get something to start with, then you can develop. So this present time has changed: the work of man-making is started side by side with the giving of the experience on the very first day. And when you see the experience—have the experience yourself—then I think you have something to stand on. There is no question of doubt. If doubt remains, it is only about how to live up to what has been given.

"Those who are in the intellectual sphere must understand the why and wherefore of things; otherwise they won't take them up. Furthermore, they will require some evidence from the past Masters and also must see whether it appeals to their common sense. If they are intellectually satisfied, then they take it up as an experimental measure. Even then, they are very skeptical: this may not be for them. But when they have something to start with, there will be more. The maintenance of diaries is necessary to 'take heed that the light'—whatever is given you at the time of initiation—'is not darkened.' This is how matters stand in the present days.''

QB: ''Master, this might seem an odd question: but, for instance, I have just recently moved to Denver, as I told you in Texas, and we don't have a group there; Mr. Poncet and I would like to start one. We meditate in my little apartment—he and his mother and I, together. Does it do any harm if you go to another group that meditates? I mean would there be any conflict of vibrations or anything if we went and meditated with another group?''

THE MASTER: ''What group?''

QB: ''Well for instance, Self-Realization. They have a group in Denver where they just meditate, and they have asked us to come for meditation. I'm not doing, naturally, any of their techniques: I gave them up several years ago when I was initiated by You. But I was wondering if there would be any conflict of vibration or anything.''

THE MASTER: ''The point is—did I tell you not to go?''

QB: ''No, You didn't.''

THE MASTER: ''Now, a further thing: if you go there, don't follow their way of meditation, but do your own. That's one thing.''

QB: ''Well, that's what I mean—that I can go and meditate in my own way.''

THE MASTER: ''Well look here, that's one thing. The other thing is, when you—those who are on the same way—sit together, there will be more radiation. Do you follow my point? There is a radiation from the Master, too.''

QB: "From Yogananda, you mean,—their Master? Would it affect me?"

THE MASTER: "Oh no, no, I am talking about something else. When you go to somebody, don't change your mode of meditation. And if you sit with those doing the same meditation, there will be more radiation. Do you follow me? I never stopped you from going any place."

QB: "No. I didn't know if there would be a conflict of vibration—if there was any from their—"

THE MASTER: "Don't you follow now what I said? If you think of Swami Yogananda there, then there will be conflict. Because Yogananda is not there. Do you see?"

COMMENT: "That follows the principle then, Master: 'Where two or more are gathered together in my name—' "

THE MASTER: "Listen—'In my name.' "

COMMENT: "That's right—'in my name.' "

THE MASTER: "You've got it. I don't mean in any way to reflect on Swami Yogananda. I don't mean that. One is a living force—radiation—going on throughout the world. When one or two sit in His name, there is radiation. Those who are higher, who have left their bodies, have to work through the human pole working on the human plane. Do you see? That is the law. I never stopped anybody from going anywhere. But I did suggest to you that when there is a group meeting, you must attend it, because you will benefit by the radiation."

QB: "Well, I hadn't gone, but I was just wondering about it."

THE MASTER: "Now the matter is clear. But I never stopped you from going there. Understand the principles, you see. I will tell you what the old Egyptians used to do. They gave initiation; they gave the way. They did not give experience, I tell you. They just put them on the way intellectually and then told them to remain quiet for two long years. They were called *mystes.* And by putting in two years regularly on the way, naturally the way opened up; sometimes there were flashes. When the inner way was opened, they were called *epopteias.* Now the way is opened the very first day! You see the light; you have some experience.

"The best thing is, when you are initiated, don't talk to anyone. Work for your daily livelihood. As for the rest, you need not talk to anyone. Talk to your Master. We talk to others. What loss is there? You talk to others: you want to show your superiority to others. Egoism is there, and you lose. Suppose, in a worldly way, you have a friendship with somebody, a love for somebody: you wouldn't dare to let anybody know about it. Is it not so? Why? This is love. Why should you broadcast your love for God? You only want someone who can guide you. And it is the Master who can guide you. He does not say that you should leave your work. Earn your livelihood, bring up and nourish your children, keep up your body, and go on with it. Let the wild flower grow in darkness. We throw seeds anywhere: 'I am doing it'; 'I see that I am in a very intoxicated state.' Others naturally ask why. You say, 'Well, when I sit in meditation, this and that appears.' Their eyes are on you. And you have not yet become perfect. What happens? They take you as the ideal. You stand between them and the Master. Where will you go? The man who follows you and takes you as a wrong ideal is first doomed, and your progress is retarded. This is a very critical point.

"In a worldly way, when you are engaged or betrothed to somebody you think only of him. Don't have any interest in anybody. Go on with it. You will find that sometimes people who are progressing begin to tell one another, 'It is like this.' The result is that their progress is lessened. And you will find many who say 'We had more progress before; now we have less.' And what is the reason for that? Do you follow my point? This is to be followed by everybody.

"When you are given it, go to the highest. Let others be the ones to say it. Then it's all right. If you have, for instance, a little water with you, and you begin to sprinkle it, what happens? Be in contact with the perennial source. Then thousands—millions—may come. Then you become a conscious co-worker, conscious that it is not you doing it, but God doing it. These are the little things, I think, that stand in every man's way. Those who have a little experience—for instance, they sometimes see the Master within—are, in a day or two, talking about it. Sometimes the Negative Power appears, and they are misguided. Some things come true, others become wrong.

"I sometimes get letters from people who write "Oh now the Master within me will guide me.' I tell them, 'All right, the Master is within you. If He guides you, write to me. Get it confirmed in writing by me.' And the result is that those who follow them are retarded. Do you see?

"I don't see why people are after becoming a Master. They may have that ideal before them, but they have not become Masters. When they become Masters, then let them say they are Masters. Even then they won't say it. Those who are Masters, don't say, 'We are Masters.' They say, 'It is God's power working. It is the Father in me doing it.' They never say, 'I am doing it.' The son of man is differentiated from the God in man. But others, who have just a little experience, exert themselves.

"This is one of the causes of division in the groups. Some

follow this man; some follow that man. The result is that there is a split. There is no progress. And this has also been the cause of dissension in the group, I tell you. I have watched it. Some begin to rule; still others are forceful; and naturally others disbelieve them. Then the dissension starts and the whole process is retarded. And that becomes a bad example for others.

"When you are put on the way, see where you are. Go up! Let people see only when you are in full bloom. Do you see? Don't broadcast your seeds. They will be eaten up by sparrows. Those who look to you will be having faith in you instead of the Master. They will think 'He is also as good as the Master.' The result is, that since you are not yet perfect, something wrong will come out of you; and, naturally, the whole thing will be very badly affected.

"When you are initiated, simply go on. You have been given the diary to keep. Remain in contact. If God wills it, He makes each one of you a Master. It is a selection from God, not from the men underneath: It is not a matter of voting, as you would select a minister or president. It is the God overhead. It is a commission from God. The soul trembles at considering the duty that lies on the shoulders of a Master. People think it a great privilege because they sometimes consider that other people have faith in them, and that becomes a source of income too. The result is that the one who places himself in this position is spoiled. His progress is retarded, and the progress of those who follow him is also retarded. Their ideal is changed. It is a very dangerous way.

"When you see the Master within, talk to Him. All right. Then remain in touch. Even then, I tell you, even if the Master speaks within you, you can never think: let your Master go and you remain. You see?"

QB: "I see the Master within sometimes, but He never looks at me. He is either sitting in meditation or with head bowed or something."

THE MASTER: "Just go into your diary, please. You will find the answer there. He is a very strict judge, I tell you; He does not spare me. [*laughter*] Surely, I must be truthful. Be a hard taskmaster: introspect yourself. When we write the diary, we make allowances. Treat yourself like a hard taskmaster."

QB: "That's the thing that has always confused me about the diary. That's why I—really, I'm not making excuses—but that's why I haven't kept it."

THE MASTER: "What?"

QB: "Because how can you be sure that you are being honest with yourself when you put down these things?"

THE MASTER: "I tell you, look here. When you are told to do a thing, by a Master, why do you raise questions? That's the first thing. If you don't understand something, ask Him. Why do you discontinue? That's the first thing, straight off. There is some reason for it.

"The mind is a very cunning friend. He will deceive you. He says, 'Well, look here, you cannot give all your imperfections. You are telling lies. Don't do it.' You see? 'Wait,' he says, 'When you become perfect, only then do it.' Both of you are caught. The point is, in the beginning you won't find so many imperfections within you. The more you go into it, the more you will find from day to day. Those that become more numerous already exist, but we are not aware of them. Do you follow my point?

"First your mind had to think: 'I am telling lies; I should not do it.' Then it made you leave off doing your diary.

When a thief is in the room, mind that, I will tell you, he will try to deter your attention to someone else. The thief says, 'Oh, here goes the thief; there goes the thief.' He never lets your attention be drawn to him.

"So the mind is a very cunning thief in the form of a true friend. He is like a very sympathetic man: 'Look here, why do you send in the diaries? You must become perfect first. Then send the diary—not now.' Do you see? Master said, 'Do it.' You disobey the orders of the Master and obey the dictates of your mind. If there is something that you don't follow, ask Him. There is something behind it.

"At the start I know quite fully well that you cannot note down all the imperfections of the day. Do you know the Pelman's System of Memory—the system described as 'How to Develop Memory'? Think of what you had been doing all throughout the day from the morning when you arose: 'Oh yes, I got up: I answered the call of nature; I had a bath and some food; I went to work; work was finished; and I came home.' One or two events might have come to your notice. But when you got up, what were the thoughts striking your mind? What others struck you when you were going to answer the call of nature, while bathing, and afterward? That requires going into. The more you go into it, the more thoughts you will find. In that way, one's memory is strengthened without any payment. And furthermore, our level of criterion of distinguishing right from wrong is also changed.

"The more you learn and go into the scriptures, the more your angle of vision is changed. For instance, in the beginning it might be: 'He told me lies, so I slapped his face. Oh, I did the right thing. It was tit for tat.' That's your angle of vision. You see? Later you may note: 'Oh he called me names. All right.' When you grow, you realize that when someone calls you names or tells you something wrong and you also call him names, the wrong multiplies: he tells you one thing, you say two, then comes four, then eight—like that. If you had not returned the wrong, it would have remained only one. Your angle of vision is changed, is it not? Even if you don't speak and somebody has thought evil of you, you may feel at heart: 'Oh he's a bad man.' You have a reaction. These feelings must be noted.

"There are two things: first, as you go into it, you will find a greater number of shortcomings; and further, the angle of vision is changed. This causes the shortcomings to become still more numerous. If they grow in number, it means you're progressing, I tell you: you know how many shortcomings are within you. Then, when you weed them out, they go down in number. When they are consumed, if you reflect, you can read others' minds, you can see what is going on on the other side of the wall. The purpose of maintaining the diaries is very high, I tell you.

"Don't follow the dictates of the mind. If you follow the Master one hundred per cent, only then can you have the full mystery solved. We only follow what we care to, modified by the dictates of the mind. Some follow the Master ten per cent, some twenty per cent or forty per cent: nobody obeys one hundred per cent. This is the one thing to be learned. Then when something comes up, you will say to yourself, 'Oh yes. He is within me; how can I deceive Him?' Your angle of vision will be changing; and when you are changing that way, by outer self-introspection and by coming in contact with that Power within, you'll progress like anything.

"Sometimes when Master's Form appears, He is showing His back: sometimes He keeps quiet; sometimes He is very happy; sometimes He talks to you. If He turns away His face, it means there is something wrong. We don't know why. The diary is meant for a very high purpose.

"These certain things are not given in regular talks. When you ask something, you get to the bottom of it and find out what is what. Each man has practically the same problem, perhaps in a little modified form.

"If you keep your diaries regularly for three or four months, like a hard taskmaster, you'll change. Send me the diaries blank. What greater concession do you want? Send them to me blank, and I will accept them. How long will you dare to send them to me blank?—that's the point. You cannot send them that way.

"The mind, I tell you, is a cunning thief in the form of a friend. He will deceive you in a very noble way; he appears to be very friendly. But ultimately you'll see that you are let down. When you follow, follow the dictates of Master."

QG: "Maharaj Ji, now you just gave very good examples. mostly concerning the thoughts we have."

THE MASTER: "Thoughts are very potent, you see."

QG: "Yes, well, there is, of course, pride and envy and jealousy and resentment towards others and thinking badly about others; and, of course, purity or chastity in word, thought and deed. You're sort of leading us very well; and I sometimes sit over this sheet, and I think: now what else is there that I have done wrong? And I'm just sometimes missing a clue. Is there anything else you would like to lead us to?"

THE MASTER: "That is just putting in time for meditation—coming in contact with the Light and Sound Principle within. That is what is wanted. That will help you; you will have more progress. Sometimes people bring me their diaries, and I see that their lives are very pure. They also put in two hours meditation daily. And yet there's little or no progress. I told them: 'If your diary is correct, then you should have gone to the third plane.' Do you see? Do you follow me? If our lives are quite flawless, why should we not progress, especially after putting in time for meditation? If it is due to the wrong way of doing the practice, involving breathing or this and that, it should be set right.

"We deceive our own selves, I tell you. Whatever you remember, put it down in the diary. Try to think of every thought that struck you, not what your body did. Like a very hard taskmaster, I tell you, don't spare yourself. As you don't spare your enemy, don't spare yourself. This is the most dangerous serpent in the form of a friend. He will deceive you. He will try to retard your progress and keep you led away to the negative things that will retard you from going on the way. And then, instead of seeing shortcomings within our own selves, we begin to doubt the Master. This is the work of the mind. He will do it. At least you see that there's Light and there's Sound. That much you see. Then why not progress further wonderfully? There's something wrong."

QD: "Master, what if you may have meditated when you became ill or you've been in the hospital, and you come back and you can't fill in the diary? Or take me. Suppose I was in the hospital and I could probably meditate twelve or fifteen hours, even while I was resting in the hospital. But suppose when I came home and I was recuperating—I mean, you can't go back to pick it up because you haven't had the paper with you, so you leave it blank because you don't want to put in this time."

THE MASTER: "That's all right. If for some reason or other you cannot complete your diary correctly, but you're watching your life, then you must be progressing, too. Sickness gives you more time for meditation, does it not? If you are putting in more time and there are no flaws, then you must have more progress. Is it not so? In this case you have not filled it in on account of your eyes not working; that has limited you. But the eyes won't always be like that."

QD: "No, with the eye I couldn't meditate at all—I couldn't move the eyeball."

THE MASTER: "That's all right. But still you could hear the Sound."

QD: "Yes, that came in very clear, even without doing anything."

THE MASTER: "That's only a temporary, short period of difficulty that we have sometimes. Moreover, I tell you, no matter how painful it may be, if you are trained in a way to control your attention the pain won't affect you. That is when you're developed. Feeling comes only when the attention is there. For example, when you have to have an injection, if you just control your attention, it is not so pinching, not so painful."

QF: "Master, I have another question: it joins on what you were saying."

THE MASTER: "Yes, yes, most welcome."

QF: "You say how our minds can deceive us and lead us away from the direction. Yet one does not want to enter into this as a purely emotional experience. Well, then how am I to come to decide, to judge? I have to use my mind."

THE MASTER: "You'll get help! You'll get help."

QF: "I see. But earlier you told me I must not expect to be able to understand and rationalize everything."

THE MASTER: "Yes, intellectually you must grasp the theory. The work that has to be done by a learned man and an unlearned man is the same: you have to withdraw your attention from outside, still your mind, still your body and analyze yourself from the body. That's a practical thing. A learned man says, 'Why should I withdraw my attention? What result will I get?' There are two men: one is learned, the other is unlearned. If you order them, 'Go up the stairs,' the learned man says, 'Well, how many steps are there? Well, if I reach such and such a place, what will happen? If my foot slips, then who will save me?' He will consider so many things. The man who is unlearned, he'll run up.

"A learned man must understand, for only then will he start. The other does not need all that botheration, I tell you. He will go ahead at once.

"Two men, one learned, the other unlearned, went to a Master to be put on the way. The Master told the learned man, 'I'll charge you a double fee.' And to the other man who was unlearned, he said, 'I'll charge you only a single fee.' The learned man said, 'Oh, I know so much, I'm so learned, why are you charging me a double fee?' The Master told him, 'Well, I have to first make you unlearned and then you will do it.' [*laughter*]

"Both have to do the same thing. The difference lies only in that a learned man who has inner experience will explain it in so many ways. Even an unlearned man who goes up, takes you up. He may not be able to quote from so many past Masters, or draw so many inferences, but he will give you this thing and he will quote only from the vocabulary of the environment of which he is in command. Christ spoke in the parable of the farmer who sows seeds: the seeds that fall on stony ground don't grow; those that fall in the hedges grow, but are retarded; those that fall on the prepared ground will grow. Consider how he even quotes this example. Masters never were educated in any college or university. Do you know in which college Christ read or Guru Nanak read or Prophet Mohammed read? Do you know of any college? I don't think so. It is an awakening from inside. They see. It is not a matter of inferences, feelings or emotions: it is a matter of seeing. They see, and they make others see."

QH: "Master, may I ask a question?"

THE MASTER: "Yes, surely, like an attorney. Even God is afraid of an attorney, I tell you." [*laughter*]

QH: "Master, before I ask it —"

THE MASTER: "No, no, you are most welcome. I'm just—I'll tell you a story later on —"

QH: "The Master is a great scholar, as we know."

THE MASTER: "Is it?" [*laughter*]

QH: "I'm sure His academic attainments have not thwarted His spiritual path. And therefore I would say that intellectual accomplishments can very often be helpful."

THE MASTER: "Intellectual attainment is the garland of flowers around the neck of a practical man. He will explain things in so many ways. Whatever way he takes up, he will tell you something to prove it: at the level of common sense, too. But a learned man without any experience is something like a library only. There may be so many things in the brain; but to have libraries there cannot give you any practical experience. Learning is good, you see; I'm not denouncing it."

QH: "Well, now, I'm going to take the risk of asking a second question."

THE MASTER: "All right, come on, please."

QH: "Which probably is an intellectual question, but it bothers me."

THE MASTER: "Well, I will answer it to the best I know how."

QH: "And it is prompted by the discussion of this sister here on Yogananda. Now Yogananda was a great yogi. And in the Master's book, *The Crown of Life*, the Master touches on this very subject in pointing out the highest plane of the yogis. And then he goes on to discuss four additional planes: Sach Khand and the three higher planes beyond that. It would be very helpful to me, Master, if you would touch on the subject and tell us a little about those four planes."

THE MASTER: "I tell you. You would like to know about those planes from where—from the yogis' point of view? From which point of view?"

QH: "These are the four planes that the Master discusses which are above the highest plane of the yogis."

THE MASTER: "I tell you. There are stages of yogis, too. Some are *yogis*, some are *yogiraj* or *yogishwar*: there are two stages of yogis. *Yogis* generally go to the first plane—*Sahasrar* or *Suhansdal Kamal*. A *yogishwar* goes to the third plane and dips into the beyond a bit. And the *Sant* is one who reaches *Sat Naam*, the true home of the Father, or true Father, you might say. There is also the *Param Sant* who transcends even those three higher planes and becomes one with the Wordless. These are the stages. There are many people belonging to the first stage and some to the second or third. There are few who really have transcended beyond the three. Those who are regularly in the fourth plane are called *Sants*. The fourth plane is divided: some people mingle it into one, some into two. The true plane of Sach Khand—whatever it is called—is the stage of full effulgence of the wordless God into expression. And in the further stages there is absorption: *Alakh, Agam, Anami, Soami, Radha Soami,* or *Nirala,* or *Maha Dayal,* or whatever they are called. That is the stage of the highest, termed *Param Sant.* The *Satsang* path is that, you might say, of the Param Sant. So that's the difference.''

QH: "Now my limited intellect can almost picture Sach Khand, which the Master describes as pure spirit. But then the Master goes on to describe three planes above the planes of Sach Khand. which itself is pure spirit, and that's hard for me to —''

THE MASTER: "No, no. Mark the difference in the words that I am using. I've said that Sat Naam is the *full expression* of the Wordless state of God: He is fully expressed. In the higher planes, the soul goes on being absorbed until it comes to the Wordless state, where there's no Light nor Sound. Those are the above stages. Ultimately, in the Wordless stage, there's no expression of Light or Sound. That comes only when it comes into expression. There are different divisions, you might say, of Sach Khand: *Alakh, Agam,* and the ultimate, wordless state that is called Nameless One, *Maha Dayal, Radha Soami*, and by so many other names.''

QH: "Well, then, Master, would *Agam* be the first stage of manifestation?''

THE MASTER: "Generally, that power which is in full expression takes the form of a Guru. He is the Sat Naam working within the human pole. Then Sat Naam comes to absorb you further. So a Guru also has stages: *Guru,*

1

2

3

4

5

Ruhani Satsang

KIRPAL SINGH
FOUNDER & DIRECTOR
INTERNATIONAL HEADQUARTERS
SAWAN ASHRAM
DELHI 6, INDIA

Dear Russel –

I was shocked to learn how you left for San Francisco without seeing me – I have so much love for you, and have great appreciation of the sacrifice of you both that you have been making by leaving your health & home and accompanying me throughout – I was wondering if you may not be financially in any stringency – I have love for you and you are on my mind – Be rest assured – I would love you to be with me – if otherwise not inconvenient to you. With all love. Yours Affly Kirpal Singh

6

7

8

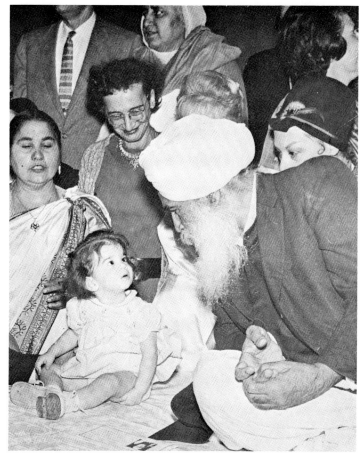

9

10

12

13

14

15

17

18

Gurudev and *Satguru*. A *Guru* is working at the human pole, but it is God in him Who is working: he is conscious. *Gurudev* manifests when you rise above the physical body. That works in the second to fourth planes, up till the fifth. to absorb you in the Sat Naam. *Gurudev* means 'The Radiant Form of the Master.' Then Sat Naam is the true Satguru. That absorbs you by stages: *Alakh, Agam*, like that. So there are stages of the Guru, too.

"Everybody is called a Guru, but Guru is the name given to such a person at whose human pole God is working for the guidance of mankind. Sometimes He is loving: sometimes He says, 'All right, don't do it,' as an average man would. But inside He is fully conscious; He gives you the right guidance. And when you rise above the physical body, He comes to you in the Radiant Form called *Gurudev*. *Gurudev* means 'Effulgent Guru,' you might say. That guides you in the higher planes—the second, third and fourth—and absorbs you in the Sat Naam; and the Sat Naam further absorbs you in the Wordless state. But people generally make no difference: they say everybody is a Guru. Do you follow me?

"These things are given in the scriptures, but they are not differentiated. That's the pity. We are not convinced unless we begin to see for our own selves. There was one devotee named Indra Mati, who lived in the time of Kabir. She went to the fifth plane and saw *Sat Purush* as Kabir. She told him, 'Well, Kabir, if you were Sat Naam yourself, why didn't you tell me before?' How many are there, even now, who think Master is a Master? When everything goes all right, according to your own wishes, you say, 'Oh, Master is great: Master is greater than God.' And if anything goes against your wishes: 'Oh, what kind of Master is that?' The flaw may be lying within you or you're not putting in regular time for meditation. And you say, 'Oh, Master has failed.' *You* are incompetent."

QB: "As a matter of fact, Master, I don't want to take any time; but very apropos of that, two years ago, when I was still in New York and attending the Satsangs there, I slipped on the ice and broke my left arm. One of the persons attending the Satsang in New York said to me (I don't think she was initiated but she had been coming there), 'Why, I can't understand how you broke your arm when you've got a Master.' And I said, 'Well, it could have been a worse thing. He saved me from—from breaking my back. I got rid of karma fairly easily.' But she was quite indignant: how could anything happen to me when I had a Master?"

THE MASTER: "Master is there to wind up your actions—to wind up the whole account, like a bank which fails. Winding up, I tell you. The many things that are here brought into fruit sometimes make your soul stronger, too, and they lose all pinching effects. When you become selfless—well—you are saved. That's all."

QB: "Well I was very grateful. I said, 'Well it could have been my back or my hip, but it was just my arm, I got off very lightly.' "

THE MASTER: "When a man is initiated, he should go on sincerely with it. He has no concern with anyone except the Master. Go on. When you get something to start with, what more proof is required? As you progress inside, you will be more convinced. But when we have a little progress, we sometimes are puffed up: 'Oh, I know this—then do it'; 'I tell you, look here, do that thing; for if you don't, I'll curse you.' And what is the result? The whole science is lost, I tell you. And such people become a defamation of the teachings. Go on with it. Any difficulty that you have will be solved of itself, unasked for."

One evening after Satsang Master called another Satsangi and me to discuss a particular point which I do not now recall. When we had finished, and the other Satsangi had left, I was alone with him and Tai Ji, who was resting on the floor in a corner of the room. He was reading a letter from Nina Gitana of Kirpal Ashram, and commenting on it out loud. At one point he said to me, "She has two cats!" and chuckled. When he finished, he turned to me and said gravely, "She should be here with me. Why is she not here?" I said, "I don't know, Master; maybe she can't afford it." He looked at me: "I will pay her way! Has she got a telephone?"—"Yes, Master. I think she does." "Then call her, please, tell her I want her here with me and I will pay her way."—"Yes, Master." I did get Nina on the phone, after some difficulty, and gave her Master's message: she said she would come immediately but it would not be necessary for Master to pay for it. I went back in. Master was sitting on the bed. He looked at me. "Where is your wife?"—"Downstairs, Master."—"Call her. Tell her to come up." I conveyed this to someone outside the door and went back into his room. He said, referring to Judith, "She is a loving soul, you see." I agreed: "Yes, she is." Just then she came running in, breathless, her dear face anxious and excited. Master looked at her, his face stern. "What do you want?" he said to her for all the world as if he was horribly displeased with her for barging in on him. She stopped dead. She looked at him first, then at me, then back at Master: "But I thought—they said—" Master shook his head. "What do you want?" he repeated, his face expressionless. Judith was totally bewildered. So was I. A little trace of a smile began in the corners of his mouth and slowly slowly his face cracked and melted into a loving smile. Gently, I would even say sheepishly, he said, "I was just joking, you see." Then he spoke with us intimately about many things, including how much money we had spent following him: $1,100. He shook his head: "So much money! You must stand on your own feet."

Day sped after day, and before it seemed possible it was the 29th of January—the day the Master was leaving. He had been the focal point of our lives since September 1; our existence was measured by His Light—and now he was going. It was true that he had stressed more and more as the day of departure grew closer that the real Master was not the body but the Power working through the body; that what we were able to perceive through the lens of his body was only a tiny part of the whole of the Reality which that Power was; that if we would just develop receptivity to that Power, we would enjoy the same relationship with It as with the physical human being called Kirpal Singh: and physical distance was not and could not be a factor since that Power was within us. We knew that this was not only all true but a cornerstone of Sant Mat; nonetheless we were sad, because we also knew that the joy and peace and fulfillment that comes from physically sitting at the feet of the living Master is a unique thing in this world and we were about to lose it. Being with him made so many things self-evident: watching him move, hearing him talk, observing (insofar as we could) His essence, it was not necessary to read libraries full of books to discover the purpose of human life. It was only too clear that the purpose of human life was to become just like Him.

There is a well-known story in India about a lion cub that was trapped by a shepherd and brought up with the sheep, so that it naturally assumed that it also was a sheep. Bleating and eating grass, it passed its days until a lion came along and saw what had happened: taking it to a stream, the lion made the cub look at both their reflections and then roared . . . Truly, this is the primary function of the Guru: to make us see what we really are and to encourage us to act accordingly. This he does by showing us himself.

The Master gave us a brief farewell talk in Mr. Khanna's living room where so many beautiful Satsangs had been held. After the talk I was standing in the hall, thinking on the implications of the day. Master came up to me, looked into my eyes with more love than I had ever seen from anybody—more love than I would have thought human eyes could contain—and said my name so that it sounded like a caress, two or three times. Then he gently slapped me on my cheek—over and over again, first one cheek, then the other—all the time repeating my name. The slaps were very gentle; it would be as accurate to call them vigorous pats. Time stood still for me while He was doing this: caught up in His Love and lost in His eyes, I forgot everything but Him and His love for me. I don't know how long we stood there.

Eventually the long drive to Kennedy Airport in New York was underway (yes, we were driving to Kennedy from Washington). We drove to Staten Island via New Jersey and took a ferry to Long Island; it was obvious that we were late. Just as the ferry was pulling into Long Island, and we were poised ready to drive off, the Master's car pulled up beside our own. Mr. Khanna leaned out to speak to me: "We are late," he said. "Will you please stop at the first telephone, call the airline and ask them to hold the plane for a few minutes? If you do that we might make it." My heart sank down to my feet. I knew that meant that neither I nor the others in my car would see the Master again till God knew when; obviously by the time we reached the airport, he would have already boarded the plane, since it would be held especially for him. Oh me. I looked at the Master; he was waiting for my answer, and it was clear to me that he wanted me to telephone. "Yes, I will do it. I will certainly do it," I said, although the collective sadness in the car hung heavily around me. I drove off the ferry, stopped at the nearest pay phone, got through to the airline, made my request and got an agreement from them. Then—

Then I went back to the car. It was pouring rain. I sat behind the wheel and my whole self rose up and protested over not seeing the Master one more time. Tears rose. "I must see him again," I thought, "This can't be the end. It *can't* be. Oh Master Master I must I must I *must* see you again. Oh Master please!" I started the car and drove onto the road. It was dead silence in the car. No one spoke. The windshield was awash with rain and my eyes with tears—between the two I could hardly see; but faster, faster, faster I pushed the car, praying all the while—"It can't, it can't, it can't be over. There must there must there must be one more time. Please Master oh please if you love me a little—just a tiny bit—please please please"—all I knew was that prayer and the gallons of water everywhere and the grim fact of driving.

When we arrived at the airport I parked and we ran breathlessly to the building, hoping to get one last glimpse of Him before the plane took off—if indeed it had not taken off already—when to my astonishment I noticed several disciples standing around the door. What were they doing there? Why were they not inside seeing Him off? Did that mean He had gone? My heart drooping, I grabbed one of them—an Indian—and asked breathlessly, "Where is

He? Has He gone?'' He looked at me strangely and said. "Yes, he's gone," and my heart sank down as far as it could go, and I surrendered to despair. Thirty seconds later it became obvious that there had been a misunderstanding for incredibly, impossibly, the Master's car drove up to the door and He got out, gave us smiling darshan, and walked into the building. Almost immobilized with joy, we followed Him in.

Piecing it together afterward, this is what happened: the driver of Master's car had, due to the blinding rain, three times missed the turn-off to the airport and *three times* drove around its entire circumference before finally making the correct turn. The airline had held the Master's plane fifteen minutes beyond take-off time, but when he still didn't show up, it finally left (this is probably what that disciple thought I had asked him). So—after some arranging, Master and his party caught another plane half an hour later, going via Frankfurt rather than Rome, and he gave us darshan for that time. Then he said goodbye and was gone.

3. Subsequent Meetings

The next time we saw the Master was a little over a year later, February 1965, in India. In those days, very few American disciples made that journey; I'm not sure why, except that jet planes were still new, the trip was much more expensive then than it was later, and it had just not penetrated our consciousness yet that we could go. We went (Judith and I) in 1965 because the Master had issued a general invitation to all his disciples to attend the Third World Religions Conference to be held in Delhi on February 26, 27, and 28. This Conference was being sponsored by the World Fellowship of Religions, an international organization of which the Master was President. Judith and I cared very little about the Conference, but we cared very much about seeing the Master again, and the invitation made our longing multiply many times. We were there three weeks; and that trip, our first to India, was very difficult for us. We were not at all prepared for the reality of India, and a profound culture shock set in: everything and anything bothered and irritated us. A week after our arrival we both came down with dysentery, which kept us flat on our backs for a week and weakened us for the rest of the stay; and because of the Conference, not only were we coming and going constantly, but the Master was also so very busy that we seldom got to be near him for more than a few minutes at a time. He was aware of this and was very kind to us in many little ways; he took us to his retreat in Rajpur, near Dehra Dun, in the foothills of the Himalayas, for the last week of our stay. Here also however he was still very busy with the overflow from the Conference, so that we saw relatively little of him even there.

Still many memories of those three weeks, which seem now so very long ago, jostle each other to come forth: the revelation, for example, of seeing the Master interact with his Indian disciples, a very very different group than the Americans: they would invariably try to touch his feet when they greeted him, and he would invariably stop them. The disciple would begin to drop down, and the Master, watching for this, would drop even faster, so that he would catch the disciple about halfway down. This little maneuver was always executed with a generous good humor that never failed: even in his eightieth year it was there. Another characteristic reaction of the Master that I observed for the first time on this trip was the way he refused garlands. In India it is very common to garland people (that is, throw long ropes of flowers around their necks) on any excuse; we were garlanded when we arrived at the airport by the people who had come to meet us. The Master was constantly being garlanded for some reason or other, except that he would never accept them. He would arrest the garland in its descent and very quickly, before the other man could grasp what was happening, he would put it around *his* neck—the man who was trying to garland the Master! It was very funny to watch.

Other incidents stand out in sharp relief: Hearing the Master, talking to someone in the room next to ours at the Ashram, say, "I want you to be a Buddha—not a Buddhist!" which, I thought at the time, seemed to sum up the essence of his teachings as well as any one sentence could; arriving at the Ramlila Grounds on the first day of the World Religions Conference exhausted, frightened and unnerved after our first bout with an Indian crowd, and seeing the Master go out of his way to walk over and check on us, saying with twinkling eyes, "You are all right? You are not dead?" which made us laugh and restored our perspective and made us love him more than ever; the seriousness of his reply to one of the Conference delegates who had asked him if a certain man was his disciple: "I have no disciples. Only God has disciples. They love me and I love them. They are my equals, and I treat them that way"—contrasted with the lightness of the afternoon in Rishikesh when the Master casually tossed a toy scorpion into the lap of Bibi Hardevi and then roared with laughter when she shrieked in surprise; and that same afternoon in Rishikesh, our memorable first meeting with the Maharishi Raghuvacharya, a venerable holy man at that time 108 years old, who was not only one of Kirpal Singh's leading disciples but perhaps his closest friend.

By the time it came to leave, our culture shock had evaporated and we felt that Sawan Ashram was truly our home; and our farewell interview with the Master was specially moving. As we left the Ashram I felt a deep deep grief which continued till long after we got home.

The years following were formative: the Ashram that Kirpal Singh had founded on our farm slowly and painfully began to take shape, and the local nucleus of initiates just as slowly increased. To manage an Ashram was not a task especially congenial to either Judith or me; it was not what either of us would have chosen for a lifework. We were—and are—both essentially private people, not at ease with more than one or two persons at a time, and loving regularity and the knowledge that when the day was over we would be alone and free. Well, that wasn't meant to be: the days were never over, and before there was a sizeable community at the Ashram, there was no one but us to handle visitors who turned up in the middle of the night, seekers who arrived with no notice prepared to stay indefinitely, etc. Gradually, by trial and error, we learned how to cope with the infinite variety of tests and challenges that confront the budding ashram-proprietor. We made some horrendous mistakes, certainly; when I think of some of the things I have said and done, absolutely convinced I was right, I shudder; but despite the mistakes the Ashram emerged as an entity, and the group of initiates centered around it increased from three in 1963 to about twenty-five in 1969.

Midway through this period, from the fall of 1967 to the spring of 1968, I became terribly depressed. Nine years after my initiation, I realized that I was not progressing in meditation, and had made no appreciable progress in three years. In fact, to a great extent I had lost whatever I had once gained. By this time, my responsibilities as a representative of the Master had increased, not only because the Ashram and the local Sangat were growing, but because I was now authorized to convey the initiation instructions to those persons who had been accepted by the Master. This was a great honor and responsibility; I appreciated the honor but felt the responsibility very keenly. I was attacked by guilt feelings over being an unworthy representative. I was acutely aware of my failings as a disciple and felt like a stinking hypocrite whenever I held Satsang; and every time I failed in keeping any of the commandments, it just added fuel to the fire. I managed to work myself into a neurotic mess and almost threw away (again) everything I had been given; but the love, understanding and patience of my wife Judith and the Master's letters to me combined into a stronger force working in the other direction. I was very frank and open in my letters to him and did not pretend I was feeling differently than I was; and he responded by writing me letters that I still treasure. Here is a paragraph from his letter of December 2, 1966 (written before the period of greatest depression but in response to similar difficulties):

"You need not dwell much on your personal character or impurities of mind. It amounts to self-pity. You will please appreciate that by watering the seedling at the roots, the plant thrives most and blooms in abundance. The holy Naam is the tried panacea for ills of the mind. Although it is a very happy augury to be conscious of one's shortcomings, undue apprehension sometimes breeds morbidity which hampers inner progress. The conscious contacts of divinity within revolutionizes the thought pattern of the child disciple and he sees everything in much clearer perception. Slow and steady wins the race. Your job is to be implicitly obedient and humbly dedicated. It is for him to reward you for your efforts. Patience is the noblest virtue but it is the fruit of very long cultivation. Just learn to live in the living present with undivided attention and devotion. You should train your mind in such a manner that when you do anything required of you, there is no hurry, compulsion or resentment from your side. You will find that it will be helpful to you in all spheres of life including meditations. My love and blessings are always with you.''

This letter has been a constant companion to me over the years and, after Judith succeeded in helping me to change my perspective so that I was open to the Master's words again, it was enormously helpful to me in overcoming my depression.

Another similar letter, written to me at a time of great trouble and turmoil which I was compounding by making one mistake after another, was dated March 10, 1967:

''Worry and hurry are the chief causes to dwell on by the mind. If you could just eliminate these two by resigning to the divine Will and Pleasure of the gracious Master Power working overhead, you will be relieved of the undue strain and stress. Please note it for certain that whatever comes to your count is in your best spiritual interests, and to become a fit receptacle for the divine grace you have to inculcate a sense of self-abnegation and affacement without involving your mind. The more you are relaxed, reposing and receptive, the more ineffable bliss and harmony will fall to your lot. Just rise so high in the loving lap of the Master Power to consider yourself as a child, who would relish 'Not my will but Thine be done.' Your deep gratitude for manifold blessings is good and appreciated.''

And then the following, dated November 24, 1967, written in response to one of the most depressing, despairing, bottom-of-the-sewer letters he probably ever received—a terrified cry for help on my part:

"You need not be skeptic about your restricted inner progress. It appears that you have been prey to undue skepticism on your part, thereby (causing) your inability to progress more on the holy Path. Suchlike feelings not only hamper inner progress but create more confusion and retard receptivity. Your job is to be earnestly and honestly devoted to your spiritual practices, and leave the results to Him . . . It appears that you have been deluded in your way by the intrusion of these morbid feelings which has resulted in a setback. . . . You should forget all about the past and be devoted to your meditations with renewed faith and you can still have it.

"Lust and anger are human elements. These can be subdued carefully by right living as discussed in the books and letters from time to time. If you will care to take stock of things, you will find much scope of gratitude as you have improved considerably in all spheres of your life with the grace of the Master.

"As regards your working for the holy cause in the capacity as a representative of the Master, you must know it for certain that the gracious Master Power has His immaculate ways of divine dispensation. He can take work from one and all who offer themselves lovingly. If you will inculcate a keen sense of humility by self-abnegation and effacement you will enjoy more ineffable bliss and harmony. Humility is the sheet anchor with the dear ones. It is an adoration of the Saints who work in this physical plane by keeping their divinity hidden from the public gaze. How safe and sublime it is to work humbly on behalf of the Master by rolling all credit on to Him. You are a personal testimony to the sacred truth that when you work for the Master for channeling the divine grace, how graciously you are compensated. The golden principle of attributing all success to the Master Power and failure to your own personal weaknesses to be overcome gradually should be followed lovingly. Ego is a human element. It is annihilated very slowly by meditating on the Sound Current and Light principles. Gradually it will dawn upon you that you are simply a doll in the hands of divine powers, dancing to His bid . . . ."

With the grace of the Master, repeated readings of this letter, renewed applications to meditation and Judith's loving help ultimately brought me out of my depression (which no one other than Judith and the Master knew anything about) and Master's words quoted above—"Everything is still within you and you can still have it"—proved true.

As the years went on, my life changed outwardly as well as inwardly; in the summer of 1969 I made plans to leave my job as a linotype operator and open a printing business in partnership with a brother disciple. The bank loan obtained to finance the business, coupled with new low fares to India through group rates, made possible another visit to Master—this time for six weeks, and this time—reluctantly—alone. Both in terms of money and of the needs of the children, Judith and I sadly decided that this time I would go without her. It was the first time in our marriage that we had been separated for anything like that amount of time, and as I left her in Kennedy Airport, on September 21, 1969, my eyes filled with tears so that I could hardly see. Waves of homesickness and loneliness for Judith and Miriam and Eric haunted me through the course of the whole flight. I remembered the difficulties of the last trip with a real sense of foreboding, and all my sins and errors of the four and a half years since I had seen the Master crowded in on me. I was afraid of a reappearance of the culture shock that had plagued us so before, and, in short, I spent the plane ride in a self-induced neurotic terror. But it ended the moment we landed.

For, by some miracle, this time, my second visit to India, I felt in every way that I was returning home. My initial reaction to the "feel" of India as we left the plane was one of love and joy. It seemed so right! Everything affected me exactly opposite from the first trip; that which had bothered me now delighted me. The crowds, the noise, the smells, the animals all over the streets, the incessant honking, the breakneck speed and ear-splitting velocity of popular Hindi —it all seemed like the appurtenances of Fairyland. I loved it all, I wanted to join with it forever.

The Master was not at Sawan Ashram when we arrived, but that was all right—he had sent us a message that he was just completing a tour of the Punjab and would be back in a few hours. In the meantime just being at the Ashram itself was knocking me out. I felt as though great waves of electricity were coming up off the ground and enveloping me. Sawan Ashram was not, physically speaking, a very memorable place. Barely two acres in extent, it was just big enough by the end of the Master's life to hold the crowds that came regularly to see him. It underwent many changes over the years, and the many brave attempts to keep it green were ultimately doomed by the pressure of thousands and thousands of bare brown feet. Still, when I crossed the bridge over the mucky stagnant river that bounded it, I felt that I was entering another world— a world out of time, the ultimate refuge—a world that was impossibly, breathtakingly beautiful. This is what I felt that September day in 1969, and every other day I ever entered Sawan Ashram—until the day of Master's death.

But that day was five years ahead in 1969, and not for one second did the thought that he could actually die some day enter my head. Even though he himself was in a car somewhere between the Punjab and Delhi, his presence was all-pervading and overpowering; hundreds of miles away, he dominated this place the way few people could even if physically present. Happiness overcame me, hours before I saw him. Although exhausted from more than twenty-four hours without sleep, it was very difficult for me to drop off; I was just too excited. Eventually I did, and woke up to discover that the Master was back at the Ashram and was waiting to see us!

I raced from my room over to his parlor where the Ashramites and Western visitors—ten or so, some of them good friends—were having his darshan. We were late. I caught a glimpse of His Face through the window and then we were in the room. Oh God! As I was staring at Him it burst over me like a thunderclap that I had totally forgotten who He was! That face—not like a face at all but like the side of a mountain—I wrote to Judith that night, "How, after looking at That Face once, can we ever do anything mean or petty or unworthy again?" How indeed? Only by forgetting—which is precisely what I had done. I felt that I was five years old, and despite urgings from some of the others, I sat down at the back—I truthfully did not dare to get too near Him. Never in my life had I been more conscious of His holiness and power. I felt that I would be electrocuted if I went too close.

He was very kind to me that afternoon—he teased me and joked with me and put me at ease, knowing well how I felt. That afternoon session was short: we were all tired and the Master too had had a long and fatiguing trip. But that evening on the porch, in the midst of the blue India twilight air, whose beauty was almost sensuous, He was really extraordinarily kind. He treated me as though I were his equal. He told everyone that I was His friend. He said to me, "This is a very auspicious occasion—that we meet again." He announced that I was an expert in printing, that I had a printing press "over there" (although I had not written him about the business), and "for that purpose he has come." The effect of the whole darshan (there were plenty of other topics commented on, of course; he told, for example, an uproariously funny but true story about a husband and wife who were both Ph.D.'s and their adventures with an astrologer of which I have forgotten the details) was surrealistic, it was so unreal. Never in all my adventures with Him had there been anything quite like this: while I appreciated beyond expression Master's kindness I understood well that this was a gift from Him and was unearned by me. Why he was giving it to me I did not understand, but I certainly enjoyed it.

One shadow cast over that heavenly darshan was the noise from the television set in the Master's parlor. I had noticed the TV that afternoon and had been shocked and disturbed: What, I wondered, does the Master want with TV? But in the wave of happiness that was washed away. Now this evening some disciples were sitting in the parlor with the TV turned on so loud it literally drowned out Master's voice at times and we were sitting three or four feet away, some of us! Sadly I thought, Even here, in the heart of the spiritual kingdom on this plane, even here in His own home, He has no peace; the Negative Power is plaguing Him here as anywhere.

(I learned later that Master did not want the television set at all, but that a leading disciple had had it installed over the Master's objections. This was an instance of a pattern that later predominated: the ignoring of the Master's wishes by people whom He had placed in positions of great trust and responsibility. Masters are not dictators, and if a disciple disobeys, and is not deterred by the Master's displeasure, the Master forces nothing. As he has said, "I have come to make friends of you—not slaves.")

The Master said to me at one point that evening, "Today you take rest—tomorrow it will start!" and looked at me very significantly. I thought that seemed a little ominous, but He added that there would be a group meditation sitting for us in the morning, and he wanted me there.

The next morning he put us in meditation in a bare room with hard floors, no cushions, and no place even to support my back. One of the disciples suggested that I might try just sitting on the floor with no support like the others, but in those days I didn't think that was important. I sat on the floor all right—there was no place else I could sit—but I worked out, with great effort, a jerry-built, very unsatisfactory arrangement that supported my back but also hurt—almost immediately after I started sitting.

But it didn't matter. It didn't matter because the Great Giver, Who had given me so much already in such a ridiculously short time, was not finished: just after he ended the meditation instructions, when our eyes were already closed, he walked over to me and very gently put His hand on my head, with two of His fingers touching my two closed eyes. The second those fingers touched me, BANG!—it started! Instantly I was in the presence of the Master within and the next hour (or whatever time it was) was like a cosmic game of hide and seek—the Master laughing at me, teasing me, loving me, disappearing, appearing again, sometimes appearing twice at the same time, sometimes appearing with Baba Sawan Singh, His Master—but all the time laughing, teasing, loving, till it seemed that there was nothing else and that there had never been anything else than that blessed game with His Real and Radiant Form within. Such incredible aching happiness I had never known in my life before, even at His Feet! When the sitting was over, He asked me what I had experienced, and I told Him; but I realized as I told Him that He already knew it all anyway.

I reflected long and deeply on this, because it brought home to me more than ever before the truth that success in meditation is a gift of the Guru, and nothing that we can bring about. For four and a half years, much of that time under extreme mental difficulties, I had been sitting in meditation and had never experienced anything like I had this morning (and in fact, so strong was that gift that for the entire six weeks of my stay with Him there was not a day when I did not have the company of the Master within). Yet literally at His touch the tenth door flew wide open and I saw. But I also realized that the gift doesn't come into a vacuum—that without the years of struggle, despair, failure, and renewed effort that had preceded that morning, it wouldn't have happened. The disciple has to work hard, but still he does not *earn* anything; all he can do is put himself into a place where he can receive that which the Master wishes to give him.

That 1969 trip still seems like the high point in my life—high in every way. I was high for six weeks almost non-stop (there were a few breaks, but it is very hard to remember them now). Nothing bothered me, everything

seemed marvelous. Several days after we arrived I was
awakened about 1:30 a.m. by the noise of dogs barking—it
sounded like fifty of them. When I realize what it was,
I smiled happily: "This too is a gift from Him." Then I
started laughing as it went through my mind what my reaction would have been had I been back home!—I would have
gotten up, gone out and *done something* about it. I laughed
myself back to sleep, the sweet remembrance of Him
brushing my eyes.

There were two lines of action that the Master pursued
with me during the first weeks of my 1969 stay. One had to
do with the magazine *Sat Sandesh* and with printing his
books in general, and the other with the management of
Sant Bani Ashram. The latter surfaced first, with a question
that I asked him at evening darshan: "Do I have the right to
ask people to leave the Ashram if I feel that their staying is
working against its purpose?" (I asked him this because
there had been a few ugly incidents over the years, one of
them just a few weeks before, of people refusing to leave
and telling me that the Ashram was God's house and I had
no right to ask them to leave.) His reply was very suppor-
tive—more, in fact, than I had hoped for: "Surely—I have
entrusted you with that task!" I was relieved and grateful.
But he went on: "If people stay there too long there will be
fighting, there will be bad vibrations in the place. One
week, two weeks, three weeks—why should anyone stay
longer?" Suddenly I felt as though the breath had been
knocked out of me: I had always been very free to let
anyone stay in the big house at the Ashram, and at this time
the house was full of people, all of whom had been there for
much longer than three weeks. Did the Master mean that
this was wrong? Tentatively I asked, "You mean you don't
want anyone to stay longer than three weeks?" He looked

at me intently. "If you have your own town, what is the use of that? And —" he leaned forward—"if anyone refuses to go, tell him *in my name* to leave."—"In your name, Master?"—"In my name." End of subject.

That night I felt sick at heart. All those people! Most of them were very dear to me. To ask them to leave! And I felt terribly depressed at having been so wrong. How could I have gotten so far away from his wishes? Late into the night I sat huddled in a little anteroom at the guest house. All the joy and euphoria of the first few days had vanished. The cold bath of his displeasure had washed it away.

The next afternoon I asked for a private interview with him. I asked him point-blank, "Did you mean yesterday that *no one* should live at the Ashram?" He said, "If they are *helping*, then it's all right. But"—with great emphasis— "*no one has a claim on it.*" He then explained to me very carefully that the purpose of the Ashram was to provide a congenial environment for people to come and meditate full time for a short while, so that they could return to their homes and jobs charged up from their stay; that if all the space at the Ashram was taken up with permanent residents, then where would the guests stay? and that the criterion to determine whether any individual or family should live at the Ashram or not was what they would be able to contribute to the Ashram, both by way of *seva* or service—that is, how badly were they needed to get the necessary work done?—and also in terms of what they added to the atmosphere—that is, if anyone's presence resulted in personality difficulties and/or fighting, he/she should leave. He explained all this very carefully and I was exceedingly grateful to him for doing so. I left his presence not only with my euphoric joy completely restored, but with a very strong impression that Sant Bani Ashram would play an important role in His work in the future, and that was why He was being so careful in His instructions about it now.

The Master also at this time asked me to edit his monthly magazine, *Sat Sandesh*. This was one of the great turning points in my life, and I will always have trouble believing the faith and trust that He so freely and undeservedly gave me—a college dropout, a competent *printer* to be sure, but an editor? Still, with His grace and more mistakes and errors of judgment than I want to remember, the magazine came out every month, and continues to this day under the name *Sant Bani* (The Voice of the Saints).

He also asked me to edit several of his books, from the point of view of the English language. This took up much of my "free" time while there, but was a blessed task for me, not least because of the many opportunities for being with Him that came with it. He asked several times how I was doing, and examined my work. He objected to my editing only once, but that was a big one.

In his book *Naam or Word* are a series of quotations from various world scriptures and testimonies of meditators from different religious traditions, all making the point that meditation on the inner Light or the Sound Current was the most helping factor in their personal experience. Among the quotations was that of a Buddhist monk who related how the sound of bells from a nearby temple had sent him into Samadhi. Now the bell sound is the first significant inner sound usually heard by the practitioner of Surat Shabd Yoga, and those who have heard it know that one aspect of this Sound is exactly like that of temple bells. This is no accident; after hearing the inner Sound, it strains credulity to believe that the outer sound is anything other than an intentional copy. But this particular quotation stated very specifically that it was an *outer* bell, and I had always wondered what exactly it proved and why it was in the book at all. So as I was going over the second edition of the book which Master had given me to use as a manuscript (the version that emerged from my editing was published in 1970 as the third edition) I simply crossed the quotation out.

When Master examined the pages he of course noticed the large deletion. "What is this?"—"Well, Master, I thought—" I explained my lack of understanding to him. He looked at me with an expression of absolute amazement that anyone could be so obtuse, and he said, very patiently, and slowly, "It was not really an outer sound. He *thought* it was. How could an outer sound drag him into Samadhi?" I felt like an idiot. I saw at once the truth of his statement, particularly since I knew from my own experience that even a fully-instructed initiate sometimes can have difficulty differentiating the inner from the outer sound. So I said, "Oh." He looked at me sternly. "Leave the quotations alone, please."—"Yes, Master."

He gave us darshan twice a day during this period— sometimes for an hour and a half at a time. In the morning he would put us in meditation, leave the room, and come back anywhere from one to three hours later, depending on circumstances. After the meditation he would give us darshan for a while. Then in the late afternoon or early evening he would give us darshan again, usually on the porch of his house. He often, but not always, separated the Indians from the Westerners for these sessions: sometimes he would take Indians first, sometimes Westerners. Sometimes these meetings were deadly serious, almost heavy; sometimes they were full of happiness and fun. He did not allow darshan sessions to be taped during this period, on the grounds that the microphone would change things. The following year he did allow them to be taped, and it did (in my opinion) change things: the transcriptions of those sessions (1970-71) can be found in the book, *The Light of Kirpal*, and while they are fascinating reading, the subjective impact of those darshans seems very different—somehow more diffused—to me than those earlier unrecorded meetings. There were not very many of us at darshan in those days—seventeen was the largest number—and the atmosphere was unbelievably intimate. Sometimes the Master would have Bibi Hardevi sing one of his own songs (rumor had it that he had written more than two thousand, although I never asked him if that were really true) and the air would taste like wine and and we would be in Fairyland indeed. Other times we would ask him questions, some of which would please him and others not—like the time we asked him if it was all right to use cushions when we sat for meditation. "Cushions!" He looked at us: "Cushions are for old people!" We were shocked. Someone said what we were all thinking: "But, Master—we all use cushions!" Master laughed and laughed.

Another time someone asked what our attitude should be toward our parents. Master said we should love them. Someone else commented that his mother was terribly possessive and wanted to live next to him and dominate him. Master said in that case he could love her from a distance. I said that my mother loved me and I loved her, but I knew that she wished that I was not on the Path. Master smiled and said. "It is *because* she loves you that she wishes you were not on the Path! She thinks, 'What is this crazy thing my son has gotten into?' It is your job to show her by your life that it is not crazy. After you have shown her by example, *then* you could talk to her about it: 'Well,

Mother, have you ever considered *why* it is that they ring bells in churches?' Like that."

Then someone asked how to deal with parents who are actively opposed to what he was doing, and who put obstacles in the way of his practicing the Path. How do we balance love and respect for our parents against our obligations to the Master and the Path, if they should conflict?

In response, the Master talked about his relationship with his own parents. He said that he loved them dearly and respected them very much; that he was an obedient son *except* when they wanted him to do something that he felt was wrong. Then he did not obey them. He gave us several instances. The first one is well known: his parents were meat eaters (the Master was brought up in the Sikh religion, and most present-day Sikhs do eat meat) and they naturally expected him to eat meat also. But he refused, even as a small child, telling his father sweetly that he did not wish to make a burial-ground out of his body.

The second instance involved the worship of the god Shiva by his parents and other family members. (Strictly speaking, the Sikh religion differentiates sharply between the three Hindu gods—Brahma, Vishnu, Shiva—and the goddess Kali/Durga, all of whom are worshiped by Hindus, and the one True God Who is held to include all the Hindu gods and be above them; and no Sikh is supposed to worship any of these gods. But in many parts of India, under Hindu influence, worship of the gods is becoming prevalent among Sikhs.) Master said that his family worshiped Shiva and had an idol erected in a sort of family altar. He said, "In the beginning I also worshiped Shiva. But later when I came to know that I should be worshiping the maker of Shiva, I left that off." His family was upset, and put extreme pressure on him to conform; but he lovingly and cheerfully refused. Then, he told us, it happened that one night that idol tipped over, fell on the floor and smashed, and when the family discovered it they blamed him! They said that his obstinacy and refusal to do homage had angered Shiva and he had smashed himself to show his anger. Master said that all of his family ostracized him for months: they refused to speak to him or to take any note of him whatever. He said, "I didn't mind. I loved them. I didn't blame them; but I was not going to worship Shiva."

His final instance occurred when he was a young man, just starting on his government career. His first day in the office was spent refusing bribes. Everyone who came to his desk tried to leave some money to make sure that his particular business would be taken care of, but the Master was adamant. "Am I not paid for the job?" His co-workers advised him to conform—"We all do it; your predecessor did it"—but he refused. In the late afternoon a petitioner wouldn't accept his refusal: he walked away leaving the coins on his desk. The Master picked up the coins and threw them after him, and the clatter of the coins hitting the floor alerted everyone in the office to what was happening. Someone informed his father, and that evening his father took him aside and told him that taking bribes was an accepted practice throughout the bureaucracy, that his refusal to do it would put a burden on all his fellow workers, and he should conform. But the Master said no.

Then he showed us the other side of the coin—the value of service to one's parents and the importance of their blessing. He said that in 1916 or 1917 his father had a severe shock and forgot everything he had ever known—even things like the names of the parts of his body. Master said that he took care of him as though he were a baby, cleaned him when he soiled himself, and taught him to speak all over again: "Finger, thumb"—like that. After some time his father had another shock which restored his memory of the past but caused him to forget everything that had happened after his first shock. But when he came to know what the Master had done for him while he was so helpless, he became very grateful; and one night, while they were walking, he asked Kirpal if there was anything he especially wanted, adding that if a father's blessing meant anything he would have it. Kirpal said, "As you know, my only wish is to find God." His father stopped dead, turned to him and said with great assurance, "You shall certainly meet God!" And the Master leaned forward and told us with great emphasis, "From that very day, I tell you, I began seeing the Form of my Master within—from that day!" (This was in 1917, seven years before the Master met Baba Sawan Singh personally.)

So many are the memories of that blessed stay. Everything seemed touched with gold to me—even the shabby squalid streets outside the Ashram, where I often walked to get a Coca-Cola or some fruit in a nearby market. One day, standing in Shakti Nagar, I watched a bus come roaring around the circle. It was absolutely jam-packed, which was not unusual, but this particular bus had people hanging outside by their hands from the window along one side of the bus!—shifting the weight of the bus so much that it was tipped high on the other side. As I stared at it in stupefied amazement, the people hanging on the side saw me, and waved their free hands, yelling and laughing in glee. That summed up for me the essence of India. What a country! Is it possible *not* to love a country where that could happen?

Sometimes as I was coming back to the Ashram after having been away for a few hours, I would think, "I am at my

Guru's feet! I am at my Guru's feet!' and I would be filled with intense happiness.

One night we didn't have evening darshan at the usual time because we were told the Master had gone to a political meeting. I was aware that Mrs. Gandhi, the Prime Minister of India, had consulted with the Master from time to time (as did both her predecessors) and we assumed that he was participating in the meeting in some way. Even when we learned that it was a huge rally at the Ramlila Grounds we still assumed he would be on the stage, because I had been present more than once when he had addressed crowds of 100,000 or more from that very platform. So we begged and pleaded to be allowed to attend the meeting, and the Ashram staff agreed. After many misadventures, including being totally lost in the vast caverns of the Ramlila Grounds, we stumbled around a corner to find the Master—sitting in the audience! Now the Master was very beautiful physically as well as spiritually. Almost six feet tall (unusually tall for an Indian), his massive face and long snowy white beard was enough to make him stand out in any crowd—apart from the radiance that always surrounded him. But this time it was not like that at all. Sitting in a seat with his knees crossed, his glasses on, listening intently to Mrs. Gandhi's address, he did not seem especially pleased to see us and gestured emphatically to us not to greet him or make any sort of fuss over him. Taking a seat, I studied him closely and I realized that he was deliberately hiding himself: having withdrawn his radiance, he was sitting in the audience like any elderly Sikh gentleman, surrounded by thousands of people who had no idea at all who he was—and this was exactly what he wanted. If I did not know him very well, I thought, I would have had trouble recognizing him. When the meeting was over, he got up and left with the rest of the crowd. We went home separately, and when we reached the Ashram we discovered that he had not yet returned.

None of us felt like going to bed until we had seen him, so we waited up. Shortly after midnight, he came in. (We found out later he had been visiting terminally ill disciples.) Stepping out of his car He was once again the King; walking past His loving children shedding light and grace as He went, He seemed to carry the Universe on His shoulders. What a metamorphosis from earlier that evening! Yet truly that had been the aberration and this was the norm. My head spinning with the wonder and power of the Guru, I finally went to bed.

Toward the end of my stay the Master took another disciple and myself on a two-day tour of some villages, ending at his retreat near Rajpur. We rode in a station wagon through rural India (my first intensive look), the Master wearing dark glasses much of the time. We stopped several times, once for Satsang, other times more informally. In the afternoon we reached our first destination: a tiny village in the middle of nowhere. After Satsang, which was held outdoors we all (the Master, Bibi Hardevi, his driver, the other disciple, and myself) retired into a nearby house, made of bricks without mortar, and with a dirt floor, to eat. Our meals were served to us on huge leaves, as is the custom in India, while we all sat cross-legged on the mud floor. After the meal, the Master lay down to rest and, following his example, so did we.

Later that evening we arrived in a small town called Kaithal, the Master's main destination, where he held Satsang that night and initiation the next morning. That night after Satsang he called the other disciple and me into his room, where we talked for half an hour. I conveyed to him a greeting from Ram Dass (Dr. Richard Alpert), who then, at the beginning of his spiritual career, had an ashram just ten miles from Sant Bani, in Franklin. The Master asked me who Ram Dass was, and I explained that he was an American sadhu who followed the vegetarian diet, had taken a vow of chastity, and had a large following among American young people. The Master commented that sadhus, even though they may take vows of chastity, are seldom chaste: that true chastity includes control over thoughts and dreams as well as conscious deeds. He added, almost in passing, that he had never had a wet dream in his life.

The next morning, after the initiation, we left Kaithal to begin the drive to Rajpur. On the way he fed my brother disciple and myself a meal of fruit with his own hands—cutting, peeling, and handing it to us. Later he gave us candy for dessert. My friend, a health food person, not realizing the value of the parshad he was being offered, turned it down, whereupon the Master offered it all to me. I, having read all the right books, eagerly lunged for it, only to discover that it is not quite that easy: I got two of the three pieces being offered, but in my great zeal and eagerness, managed to drop one piece down behind the seat, where I couldn't get it.

We spent two days in Rajpur, very sweet days; the other Westerners (fifteen or so) were there when we arrived. Not at all busy, the Master had much more time for us here than in Delhi, and we met with him about four hours a day. He sent for me often to discuss various matters concerning my new job as Editor of his magazine, so that I really saw him a very great deal. One morning he sent for me while I was still in my room (a little stone room in the rear of the house, which I loved) and he was waiting for me on the porch; he had an article that he wanted me to publish in the magazine.

I went to sit on the floor, as usual, and he told me to sit in a chair. I demurred, saying I preferred the floor. But he almost fiercely pulled a chair over and ordered me to sit in it. I did, of course; and afterward I did some self-introspection about humility. Is it more humble to cling to the outward form of humility? Or to obey the Guru? What exactly was my motivation in trying to disobey him? It is true that I derived great pleasure, and felt a profound right-ness, about literally sitting at his feet; but it is also true that on this particular occasion I was worried about appear-ances—about not appearing humble enough if anyone was looking. And while I was sitting on the chair I was very ner-vous whenever anyone walked by.

When we arrived in Rajpur, a letter was waiting for me from Judith. There had been a number of letters both ways throughout the visit but in this one she revealed to me that she was worried about my coming home because she was afraid of my generally critical attitude toward her and my bad temper. It had been a very difficult letter for her to write, that was clear, and as soon as possible, I took it to Master. I told him that I often lost my temper with Judith and that she was getting tired of it. He was not happy about it. "Well, look here!" he said, "Change places with her for a week and see how the shoe pinches! They work harder than men, I tell you: little little things, but they add up. Smiling face, kind words: she'll do anything for you. Change places with her! You'll see."

On the last morning in Rajpur I left my room at dawn and went down to a cement reservoir at the back of the retreat, where the view of the Himalayas was spectacular. The reser-voir was empty, and it was a popular place for us to medi-tate in because we had heard that the Master was very fond of that place and often sat there. I was enjoying a sweet meditation when suddenly I was pulled out; I looked up and saw the Master standing there. I was overjoyed. He looked concerned. He asked me if I wasn't cold. I said that I was wonderful—especially now that he was there. He smiled and left. I went back to my meditation, the sweetness within now doubled by the sweetness without. A half hour or so later, I was again pulled out, this time by the Master's driver, who was standing there with a tall glass of hot *chai*—tea boiled with milk and sugar in the Indian way. He cleared his throat and apologized for disturbing me, but the Master had sent me this tea—Again overjoyed, I begged him to thank the Master for me, and slowly savored my parshad tea while gazing at the incredibly beautiful Himalayas and reflecting on the sweet sweet love of the Master that expressed itself equally in great big things and in little little things. I had never been happier.

The next day we drove back to Delhi via Rishikesh, and the Master visited his disciple and old friend, the Maharishi Raghuvacharya. One hundred and twelve years old in 1969, this great yogi gave every indication of being a man of sixty-five. He had met the Master in 1948, when he was in his nineties and the Master was meditating full-time in Rishikesh preparing for the commencement of his mission. When they met, Raghuvacharya, who was a widely respected and advanced yogi, was sitting with a group of his disciples; he astounded them by getting up and bowing down to the Master. The Master in turn treated Raghuvacharya as a good friend, and while Raguvacharya did take initiation from the Master, and publicly acknowledged him as his Guru, the Master never treated him other than as an equal. To be with these two giants together was the encounter of a lifetime, and few orders have been more difficult to obey than that afternoon when He sent us off to

Rishikesh to sightsee so that He could be alone with Raghuvacharya. How I wanted to stay! But I went, as we all did, and had a thoroughly miserable time.

The last day of my stay was November 2, 1969, and it so happened that a mammoth six-hour Satsang was held that day to comemmorate the five-hundredth birthday of Guru Nanak. I woke up feeling ill, a touch of dysentery (only the second occasion on that visit that I was sick, by the way; the first also only lasted a few hours) and terribly depressed over leaving Him. These six weeks had been so beautiful, and I knew that He had once again irrevocably touched my life and it would never be quite the same again. I felt that I had been able to understand and appreciate Him on a new level, and that many things that had been obscure before were now clear. I realized that my responsibilities had been greatly increased, and I had an intuition, in fact, that they would shortly be increased still more, in ways that I could not anticipate. Sitting on the ground in the early hours of that giant Satsang, before most of the crowd had arrived, watching the Master on the dais, He seemed so humble —almost vulnerable—to me. I remembered the time he had found me meditating outdoors in Rajpur and had sent me parshad tea; and suddenly the sense of His patient, painstaking, compassionate, infinitely caring love on the human level burst over me and I began to weep—great racking sobs that shook my body as all the gratitude and love that had built up over the six weeks struggled with the deep deep grief over leaving Him and it all expressed itself at once. That night I left; I did not see Him again physically for two and a half years.

The afterglow of my experience in India lasted for some time, although I began failing in one way or another even before I got off the plane. Still, as I had guessed, there were many challenges and responsibilities that were new, and with His grace, and by clinging to the memory of Him, I was able to pull them off, in most cases with a minimum of disaster. The whole project of getting the magazine going, combined with the equally demanding challenge of starting a printing business, took up most of my time. Simultaneously, the Satsang began to grow, and before long the growth had become increasingly fast: from an average attendance of twenty-five or so in the fall of 1969, it had increased to seventy-five by the early summer of 1970. This growth continued for some time, and in July 1970 we began construction of a large Satsang Hall at Sant Bani Ashram in order to accommodate the people who were coming.

The Ashram community was also growing, despite the fact that, in obedience to the Master's instructions, I had "cleaned it out" on my return home. Actually, I had not asked a single person to leave; but I had called a meeting immediately and explained Master's wish, that living at the Ashram should be based on a strictly "seva" basis, and that Master had explained that no one should stay longer than two or three weeks unless they were necessary for the maintenance of the Ashram. Within a short time, the vast majority of the inhabitants had voluntarily left, clearing the Big House for stays by guests for retreat purposes: and when the Ashram community began to grow again (as the increased responsibilities also increased the work) it grew in family units who built their own houses and became committed to the community in a far more total way than their predecessors had been. They understood from the beginning, for example, that they were there to help, not to be helped. This was a very significant change in the development of the Ashram, eventually insuring a large number of children in the community and leading to the establishment, a few years later, of the Ashram School; and it came as a direct result of the Master's direct order—an order which, in the beginning, I did not wish to obey.

Time passed. Judith went to India for three weeks in the summer of 1970; the Satsang Hall was completed in March 1971; and by the spring of that year it was being persistently rumored that the Master would be coming soon on his third world tour. I had also gotten the impression that he would be coming soon from my correspondence with the *Sat Sandesh* correspondents in India—two women who lived at the Ashram and worked closely with the Master on translations of his talks and reports of his activities. So even though rumors were always circulating that the Master was coming and I had long since learned to be skeptical, this time I believed them—after all, it had been eight years since he had come! We were preparing in various ways for his coming when one night in late June the Master appeared to me and told me something. I could not quite remember what He said—I knew there was some blockage on my part—but because I was so sure that He was coming and because I wanted Him to come with all my heart, it was not at all difficult for me to talk myself into believing that what He had told me was that He was coming. How overjoyed I was! I felt that I was the possessor of a delicious secret. For two days I hugged myself internally and thought about how soon the Master would be with us again. On the third day the cable that I had been expecting arrived. I tore it open eagerly—to find that it said that Master was doing well after his operation June 29 and that they would write with more details. It was signed by our correspondents.

Operation? The Master? For a few minutes the gulf between what the cable said and what I had expected it to say paralyzed my brain, and I struggled to make any sense at all out of the words. Then two realizations hit me at once, hard: First, that this was what the Master had told me when He appeared to me two nights before (the evening of the operation)—He had told me of His operation and that He was *not* coming—I remembered now with a rush what He had actually said, but *I had been unable to retain it at that time* and blocked it and substituted what I had wanted to hear; and the second realization was this: that the Master (His physical form) was going to die some day. I had only briefly and fleetingly grasped this before, but now I understood that it was inevitable. I went deep deep into the forest and wept.

My experience with that particular manifestation of the Master speaking to me within taught me a great lesson: to make sure that I have *really heard* what the Master is telling me before jumping to conclusions about it. It also taught me to be healthily skeptical about other people's experiences with the Master within: if I had had an insufficient capacity to hear and had ended up deceiving myself, so could others.

The Master's operation had been a serious one—on his prostate—and he was a long time recovering. His body had been exhausted for years, of course, and he kept it going by sheer will. (As I once heard him say, "A strong horse can pull a broken cart.") Now he was a long time recovering, and it made us nervous. At last encouraging reports came back, and, after what seemed an interminable amount of time, a detailed account of his operation was sent me for publication in the magazine. As soon as I could arrange it, I made another trip to see him—my third. I left Boston on January 31, 1972, intending to stay five weeks.

I went with mixed motives. The years since I had last seen him had been good years for me, and I thought he would be pleased. My going alone, without Judith, was prompted as much by my desire to recreate my last trip (when I was also alone) as it was based on necessity. I had made many assumptions about myself and my importance to the Master and his work, and these were all shattered. The Master was very very kind to me and in many ways He gave me exactly what I wanted; but he also showed me exactly where I stood spiritually—nowhere—and He showed me just how much my wish to be there independent of Judith was worth—by making me miss her so much I couldn't think of anything or anyone else, and by calling her over from within for the final three weeks of the stay. It was a good lesson, one that I hope that I will never forget.

The following paragraphs are excerpts from a talk I gave at Satsang just after returning home in March 1972 (I was so sick at the time that I could hardly sit up, but I was buoyant with the memory of His love and infinite care):

"When you come into the presence of the Master, the one thing that's always true is that nothing is what you expect. Looking back on it, it's like a big kaleidoscope: preconceptions broken, Master's greatness shown to me in ways I never really knew before. I went there full of self-importance: I had done all this work Master had assigned to me; I awaited further assignments—that kind of thing. Well, He was not displeased with anything. He didn't say anything negative or positive. It took me a while to grasp: all He wanted to talk to me about was my own inner growth.

"He talked a lot about my ATTITUDE toward work. He said, 'When you talk to people, make sure that they understand that you are telling them from the level of your understanding only. Don't assert!' Don't come on as though Master is saying it. He said, 'Whatever you do, don't be the Master of the work assigned to you. Know you're working for someone else, never forget that!'—very strong . . .

"Before Judith came I missed her like anything, and I began to feel ashamed. Here I am with the Master, we're supposed to be above such things, attachment to wives, etc. We went back to Delhi and I was trying like anything to meditate and through the Grace of God it was not entirely fruitless. But I missed Judith so much . . . That night at Darshan on the porch, Master said to me out of the blue, 'Yes, what's on your mind, speak up, heart to heart—' so kindly. All during this time, Master was showing me time and again how He knows our innermost thoughts—it was incredible, He really knows everything. There's no doubt about it. So He pulled me out like that—heart to heart. I said, 'Master, I'm disgusted with myself because of the tiny amount of love that I have for you.' He said, 'How can you measure love—how can you measure it? It's either there or it isn't.' I said, 'When thoughts of outside things come up in meditation, my mind clings—' He said, 'Look here, when thoughts of wife and children come up, don't not love them, love them for the sake of Him Who has given them to you. Then you'll be all right.' He was so loving, so kind. Many times I would be in that kind of a state. He would just talk to me and it would be like He was washing me with the gentlest kind of beautiful water. I would be shaking with happiness after just a few words like that . . .

"Our habit, even when we're with the Master, is to think always in our own terms, so that we ask questions and conversations take place in a frame of reference that is entirely of our own making. It is very rare for Master to violate that; it's like a game He plays. If you select a frame of reference,

He'll play the game within that. But if you'd selected another one, you might find out a lot more, or if you just leave it open to Him—anything could happen. These are subtle things . . .in the Master's presence there is nothing that cannot and should not and does not lead to growth, nothing . . .

"You see, Master has two kinds of beauty. Actually, He has fifty thousand kinds; but He has two main kinds. I am talking about physical beauty. The first is his beauty near at hand, like when you're sitting on the floor about six inches away from Him, and you're looking into His face and you see every nook and cranny of the boulder that His face is, and you wonder how on earth God could create such a face as that. That's one kind of beauty, you see, and you're looking into His eyes . . . sometimes I would look into them and my eyes would hurt, and I could only concentrate on one of His eyes at a time—I could not focus on both eyes at once. And I found it very difficult to answer Him when He talked to me: I would have to avert my gaze for a second in order to make my mind work enough to come up with the answer that He wanted. Because it's really true that looking into His eyes you begin to withdraw; there's no doubt about it, the withdrawal process starts.

"The other kind of beauty is His beauty at Satsang. He's sitting up there on the dais, and you may be quite a distance from Him, no doubt, but He's sitting up there and He is a lion. That's His name, you know—Kirpal Singh means merciful lion—that's His name and that's what He is. And those days in Meerut He was sitting up there holding Satsang, and the most beautifully exquisite experience in watching Him—even if you don't understand a word—watching Him make His points with His hands, the way He'd move His head . . . Sometimes He talks for three hours, more usually two. He never stirs from His waist down. From His waist up, He's swaying. He's looking, He's darting His eyes—He looks at the whole congregation, He notices everyone. He's so ALIVE! you look at Him and the life that's coming from Him is so tangible, you think, Oh my God, how beautiful, how much beauty can there be in the world? So that's what it was like at Meerut . . .

"At Manav Kendra there's a little old woman that lives there: she looks about ninety. She's all bent over with a big hump on her back. She walks around mumbling bhajans and moves very slowly with great difficulty with steps and things. So one day we were all following Master along this path, and Master's walking very fast—He just floats along (and by the way He walks just as fast as He did before His operation, and in every way He appears to be more healthy, more vigorous, more active, and more youthful than two years ago)—anyway we were all coming along this path in a big cloud following Master and there was this little old woman up ahead, and there were three stone steps in the path and she started to go up them, with great difficulty. And Master, never even breaking His stride, just reached down and put His hand under her elbow, and it looked from behind as though He just lifted her up the three steps and set her on the top. And then He kept on going. She knelt right down on the ground and took the dust from where His feet had been and put it on her forehead. The way He did it, the whole feel of the thing, was just so beautiful . . . there were so many things like that.

"Sometimes there's a certain kind of Indian disciple who has a certain way of looking at the Master which to me is meaningful beyond words. It's a smile, but it's a smile that's so extreme that it seems like their face is going to break in two. And there's tears in the eyes along with it.

Whenever you see that expression, you know that just being with the Master is almost knocking them out. And Master was so loving to people like that—He pats them on the face, He sits right down with them . . .

"Just before we left we were up in Pathankot and I said to Master, 'I can't believe in two days time we'll be in the United States.' He said, 'Who says you are leaving, who says? You will take me with you. Wherever you are, I'll be there.' He patted me . . . It was so hard to believe that we were coming home, so hard. You live in India for a little while, even six weeks, it gets into your blood. You just think, 'Oh, India,' just like you think, 'Oh, Master,—how can you be so beautiful?' . . .

"There was a Satsang the morning of our last day, and despite the fact that I was sick as a dog, I wanted to go to it . . . In both good and bad ways, that Satsang was something. I was sick in a way that's almost indescribable. I was sitting cross-legged on the ground. In the morning it was cold, but as the day went on it got hot, and I was dressed for the cold morning, with long underwear, etc., and as the day went on I really began to stifle. Master gave the longest talk without a doubt that I've ever heard Him give anywhere—three hours exactly, of which only a phrase or two were in English. And for the last two hours of that three-hour talk I was in such intense pain that I had to sit absolutely straight because any other position put too much pressure on me . . . with all that, Master's face was so beautiful—I was sitting there looking at it, I couldn't believe it. I kept getting sicker and sicker, yet I kept looking more and more at His face and I realized I would rather be there than anywhere else in the world doing anything else. You see, you can't—pictures don't get it, movies don't get it, you have to see it with your own eyes.

"Everything about the Master is so subtle. Like when He makes a point He smiles, just a little bit of a smile, and the subtle beauty of that smile just floats out across at your heart...

"When we are at His Feet, these things are very clear; but when we leave Him and time goes by and we get involved in other things—lip service is paid, but less and less of our real heart goes to the job of finding God. The Path is a very real thing. Master wants us to grow, He wants us to break through our attachments. He wants us to love, He wants us to be happy, be jolly, and live always from the level of someone who sees that the Master is taking care of him. Because He really really is. What He doesn't protect us from is the very thing we're supposed to have . . . He showed me in a million ways He knows everything. He understands everything—our hang-ups. our attachments—He can go deep down inside our minds, He sees what is there. He loves us anyway! I said to Him the last day, 'Master you have showed me over and over again that You know every thought I am thinking, the innermost desires of my heart.' He didn't deny it; He said, 'Yes?' I said, 'And yet You love me anyway?' He said, 'Look here, if a child comes to its mother smeared with filth, what does the mother do? Does she not love it? Does she not wash it down and hug it to her breast? Does she hate him? Does she beat him or kill him?'

"There is nothing, you know, that He doesn't know about us. *He knows where we're at*. He knows it. When you're in front of Him, He knows, but He knows equally well over here. Because He made direct reference to fears and hang-ups and things like that that I had over here before I went. He knew all about them; I never talked about them, not a word, but He knew. He really is God . . .''

On the afternoon of the last day in Pathankot, Judith and I were in our room—I was wretchedly sick and she was taking care of me. I had begged her to go and have darshan, so that at least she should not waste our precious last day, but she refused on the grounds that I needed her. God knows it was true—I felt as if I was coming apart inside. It was just after the three-hour Satsang I described above, and I was, in addition to being very ill, utterly exhausted. I lay on the bed like a piece of dough—no life, no spirit, no anything. Suddenly, I became aware that it was time to go and see the Master. I got up off the bed and said to Judith, "All right, let's go over." On the way over, though, I got cold feet and began to be apprehensive: it is not a light or easy thing to knock at the Master's door and request admittance—not for me it isn't. Greatly do I prefer for Him to ask me first; then I know for certain that it is His will. So this afternoon I said to Judith, "I'm not going in unless someone in high position tells me it's all right." I was thinking of Bibi Hardevi or Master's driver. But before I even had a chance to knock, the door opened and the Master Himself was standing there: "Come in! Come in!" We went in and Bibi Hardevi was waiting, with tea—our tea!—in cups and a bunch of shawls—our farewell gifts—on her lap. The Master in His great kindness let us stay with Him all afternoon, and while He did not take away my illness—when I did leave Him I was as sick as ever—somehow He worked it so that it did not matter while I was with Him, and that love-filled afternoon in one of the farthest corners of India, that He had called me to from a sickbed, was without blemish.

The next morning we had to leave Him very early, for the eleven-hour drive back to Delhi to catch our plane home. We said goodbye to Him before dawn; the last thing He did was to give me more parshad anacin and tea. We went and sat in the car and once again I wept as though my body encased the flood. I cannot describe my feelings at parting from Him—the deep deep deep grief. It is like no other sadness in the world. It is having to say goodbye to all your deepest and most cherished hopes; it is finding your reason for existence and then saying goodbye to it; it is turning your back on your original face before you were born. Such is the true Guru, and such is the grief at leaving Him.

4. Twilight and Sunset

Despite the Master's June 1971 operation, he had been vigorous and strong throughout our stay in early 1972; but I was never to see him that way again. When we met next, the following September in Washington, D.C., he had aged a million years. What I did not know for some time yet was that shortly after we left India in March 1972, He journeyed to Rajasthan where He met with His beloved gurumukh disciple, Ajaib Singh, authorized him to convey initiation, and transferred His power to him.[6] This did not of course render Him powerless; the power of the true Master is measureless, and He could give an ocean's worth away and retain just as much. Indeed, some Masters have had several disciples to whom they transferred power. But in retrospect it can be seen that it marked the beginning of the end, and He was never quite the same after that. (It was because Ajaib Singh understood very well that this would happen that he begged Kirpal Singh not to do it, but to stay on in His body—even as Kirpal Singh had begged His Master Baba Sawan Singh.)

6. This was more than two years before his death—unusual but not unprecedented. Swami Ji transferred His power to Baba Jaimal Singh in the early 1860's, and did not leave his body until 1878. See Kirpal Singh, *Baba Jaimal Singh*, pp. 46-50.

The Master's third world tour of 1972 does not, by and large, rank high in my treasure-house of memories of Him; this is partly because His noticeable age and weakness depressed me, and partly because the huge crowds that now flocked around Him added a new—and very difficult—dimension to the whole business of seeing Him. Everything in 1972 as multiplied by ten. In 1963, one hundred persons (approximately) had met Him at the airport when He first arrived; in 1972, it was almost one thousand. This ratio continued throughout.

The first ten days or so of the third tour were spent at the home of Mr. Khanna, who was living at this time in an exclusive neighborhood in Oakton, Virginia. The neighbors objected strenuously to large numbers of cars and ragged-looking young people hanging around, so the word was out not to go there for darshan, but to be satisfied with the public meetings held at a hall in nearby Fairfax. Nevertheless the Master personally asked Judith, our son Eric, and me to come over to see Him, and we went. A very very sweet darshan it was, too. The next night there were quite a few more people there, and the third night a mob; and watching the Master I had a distinct feeling that He was not pleased with such a large number of people being there. This made me uneasy, and I resolved not to go the next night.

After Satsang the following evening, therefore, I announced in our hotel room (a large two-room suite that many of us were sleeping in) that I was not going to go over that night. Some of the people were willing to go along with whatever I did, and others were determined to go anyway, which was certainly their right and, for all I knew, their duty: who was to say I was right? They left, and the few of us remaining sat around and discussed the Path. I spoke of how the most beautiful moments—in fact, the only moments that really counted—in my life were those moments at the Master's Feet. Our dear sister Amy Hart said, "Why aren't you there now?" The second she said that, I felt as though I had been hit by lightning. I knew she was absolutely right: not only should I be there, but I *must* be there, that the Master Himself wanted me there—the same way I had known it in Pathankot, only two or three times as intense. I said instantly, "I'm going over! Anybody who wants to go can come, but I'm not waiting!" I raced down the stairs, jumped into the car and drove off—along with Judith, Eric, Amy, Shirley Tassencourt and Kathy Osinski (now Mrs. Dale Peterson) all of whom had been in the room and had also made it into the car. Like a madman I drove the ten miles or so to the house—the urgency was unbearable, and I felt that I had made a terrible mistake and the only way I could rectify it was to get there as quickly as possible. We pulled into Mr. Khanna's front yard, raced into the house—and found no one there at all—no one at all *except* the Master, sitting cross-legged on His bed and beaming at us! I didn't stop to wonder where everyone else was; I threw myself at His Feet, grateful beyond words. He said softly, "Where have you been?" I just looked at Him; what could I say? He continued, "Were you lost?" and smiled. I said, "Yes, Master—I was lost, all right, but I'm found now!" He laughed.

Then followed twenty minutes of the sweetest, most loving darshan imaginable—with just us! At the end, Mr. Khanna came upstairs; seeing us in the Master's room, he called up the others from downstairs in the basement, where every soul in the house had been waiting—except for us. Master gave them a few minutes too, then dismissed us all. I felt His love that night as much as I ever had.

In October He returned to Sant Bani Ashram[7] for the first time since His initial one-day visit nine years before. Both the Ashram and the Master Who had founded it had altered much in outer appearance: the Ashram had grown many buildings, including of course the Satsang Hall, and also a small house built especially and only for the Master's personal use as a labor of love by the devotees of the area; the Master had aged so that it was a visible effort for Him to walk around the place He had once enjoyed so much, and after a few tries He was eventually driven from one place to another in a car—over the same paths and walkways He had practically bounded over on His first visit. Nevertheless, I referred to His five-day stay at the time as "five drops of eternity" and that remains an excellent description. Despite His weakening physical condition, or perhaps because of it, His spirit burned more intensely than ever; and those five days were, in terms of Sant Bani Ashram, both a fulfillment and a foreshadow—an end and a beginning.

He was pleased with His house which had been designed and the building of it supervised by His loving disciple Tibor Farkas, a Canadian architect; He was pleased with the arrangements in general, which were made possible by the loving cooperation of so many; He was concerned about the physical comfort of the dear ones in the New England autumn, which was cold; and He was both amused and concerned about the differences between the so-called seating capacity of the Hall (maximum 300) and the numbers of people who wanted to sit in it (maximum 800). By making use of overflow places with speakers and by squeezing squeezing squeezing until it seemed as if there wasn't room

7. I am giving here a very brief personal view of this last tour. The official complete account, with many pictures, can be found in *The Third World Tour of Kirpal Singh*.

enough for another pancake in the Hall—let alone a person—we managed to fit between six and seven hundred persons inside. Whenever possible, the Master held Satsang outdoors, but it was too cold to do that at night.

The Master gave initiation the morning of the last day. He had instructed me to screen and prepare potential initiates all week long, and I had been doing so: about twenty-five persons had been accepted and we had set aside the main room in the Big House for the initiation, leaving the Hall for everyone else to meditate in. But when I arrived at the Big House on the morning scheduled, I found that the number had doubled overnight! Not only were most of these persons unknown to me—they had not been screened and some of them had very little idea of what they were doing—but the capacity of the room reserved for the purpose was nowhere big enough to handle fifty persons. The fact was that some of the people following the Master had strong views about this "screening" and they were just offering the initiation to anyone and accepting all. I did not feel that I was in a position to object but I really didn't know what to do about the space problem: if we used the Hall for the initiation, which was one obvious solution, where would everyone else meditate? I ran down to the Master's house and explained the situation to Him. We were in the living room of His house, both standing. When I finished, He stood for a few minutes, looking at me, His eyes twinkling. Finally He said. "Weed out ten." I stared, not comprehending. He repeated, a bit sharply. "Weed out ten. There are too many." I blurted out, "You want *me* to weed out ten of them, Master?" He said, "Yes, surely." Suddenly I had a mental picture of myself explaining to the people in charge, who were very self-confident and sure of themselves, that I had been told to weed out ten of the very people they had been so actively encouraging to be initiated, and I laughed. I laughed long and loud, and it was a laugh of disobedience; for with that laugh I made a choice —I decided not to do what the Master had told me to do. It would of course have been very difficult for me to have done it, and again it might well have been misunderstood by others as some kind of an ego trip. So I took the easy course, and disobeyed.

Master watched me laughing very closely for a few minutes, then He also laughed. I did not feel that He was specially surprised or angry at my disobedience; I doubt that He expected anything different. When He finished laughing, He said, "Use the Hall for the initiation. It doesn't matter about the others. They don't have to meditate this morning." The matter was settled; I had got what I came for; I went up and arranged for the initiation to be given in the Hall. But many many times since that day, especially when I have felt content with myself, complacent, like a good obedient disciple worthy of being emulated by others, I remember very clearly the Master standing there, saying, "Weed out ten," and me laughing and refusing to do it, and I know that I do not have even the beginning of an inkling of what obedience means, or what is meant by self-surrender.

After the Master left Sant Bani Ashram, we followed Him everywhere we could. Beautiful intimate loving sessions in Burlington, Vermont, and Denver were exceptions, not the rule; and the physical difficulties of traveling nonstop by car in a futile attempt to keep up with the airplanes was far more difficult for me now than it had been nine years earlier. In Los Angeles, the Master spent a lot of time in the company of Yogi Bhajan, which some of us resented; we wanted Him to spend it in the company of us, no doubt.

One sweet afternoon at the home of Lucille Gunn in Glendale, the Master was asked why Yogi Bhajan, who lays so much emphasis on the Sikh Gurus and their writings, should teach Kundalini Yoga which is explicitly condemned in these writings. The Master laughed gleefully: "I don't know! Ask him." Someone else asked Him why Jesus was the only Master who had died for the sins of the world. He laughed again, not so gleefully this time: "All Masters have died for the sins of the world."

The tour continued through Dallas, St. Petersburg, eventually Fort Lauderdale. It seemed as though it got harder and harder to get to Him at each place. In Fort Lauderdale, the last stop, the crunch was immense: it was His last stop in the United States and people came from everywhere to see Him for one last time. The numbers were so many and the difficulties so multiplied that I almost gave up but not quite. One day was set aside for the disciples and the Master to be together at Birch State Park. It was a lovely day, beginning with meditation and darshan. Private interviews followed. At some point I was wandering alone in the Park when, as I was crossing a road, I met a friend in his car. He invited me to accompany him while he returned to his hotel (which was also Master's hotel) on some errand or other. I accepted. As we left his room and were standing by the elevator, I had a sudden impulse and said. "Suppose we push "5" (the Master's floor) instead of "1", and see what happens?"—Always adventurous, he said, "Fine" and pushed "5". We arrived at Master's suite to discover it almost completely deserted—everyone was at the Park. Only the Master Himself and one attendant were there. The attendant met us at the door. "Oh, good!" he said. "The Master wanted to see you. Here—this is for you!" and gave me a fuzzy Polaroid picture of Master and Yogi Bhajan sitting on a brass bed at the Yogi's headquarters in Los Angeles. I didn't like the picture and I was still feeling unfriendly toward the Yogi, so I took the picture, resolving mentally not to publish it or do anything with it. I put it in my pocket and my friend and I went in to see the Master who was sitting on His bed. He smiled and said to me, "Do you have something for me?" I could not think what He meant, unless it was the picture that I had just been given, so I pulled it out of my pocket and gave it to Him. He smiled, took it, and then proceeded to autograph it!— thus turning it into a valued possession, and handed it back, saying flatly, "You will print this in *Sat Sandesh*." I said, "Yes, Master," and I did.

On one of the last nights in Florida—possibly the last night, I'm not sure—He gave a remarkable talk on "The Coming Spiritual Revolution" which was one of the first indicators that He might be leaving soon. Especially beautiful and significant is this section:

"Every human being has a secret chamber within himself, which is called the 'closet of the body.' That is higher than the mind and heart both, and provides mind with understanding to a certain extent, and the heart with feelings of love. This chamber is the Kingdom of God within us. This is the crest jewel, the pearl of great price. The Saints, when we come in contact with them, open this chamber by withdrawing all our attention from outside. The test of a true Master is the fact that in his company, the smallest realm opens up within us, and the Light, Divine Light, the God-into-Expression Power, is seen. Christ said, 'If thine eye be single, thy whole body shall be full of light.' Prophet Mohammed said. 'The light of Allah is found where? In the human temples.' Why am I quoting these things? Because right understanding was given by Saints and Masters coming from time to time. Lord Krishna said, 'I will give you divine light and you will see my glory within.' Buddha said the same thing: 'Every man possesses the bright mirror of illumination.' This, all the Buddhas realized. Buddha further proclaimed that, 'The way of the illumined ones is the growth of snowdrops behind the eyes'; and then Christ came, and it was as if a few crocuses opened their eyes to the winter sky. But now the time has come when we can have a rebirth; this is what Christ spoke of when he said that the poor in spirit shall inherit the Kingdom of God.

"So springtime is upon us now; there will be more fragrant Saints, I would say now, who will come up and give us through the grace of God, a contact with the God-into-Expression Power. And this is the revolution, the spiritual revolution, which is coming up—an awakening all around. Why are all these people coming, you see? In the past, these things were told in the ears of the disciples after a long time of testing. Now it is given out from open platforms; people are having it without distinction, whether they are ready or not ready, they are getting something. This is what is needed—the times have changed now. And Masters come from time to time to bring these things into the experience of others who are born as human beings . . ."

These were among the last public words He spoke in North America. But on his return to India He spoke in the same vein. At the celebration of his 79th birthday (February 6, 1973—He was born in 1894, but in India they called it the "80th") He said among other things, the following:

"The fact is, all credit goes to Him (God). It is all His grace working. I said in the morning session that the sun is about to set. Take heed before it is too late . . Wake up before it is too late. You cannot depend on life.''

And on another occasion, at the same celebration:

"We have to do our work during the day. When the night falls, who can work? This is what Christ says, 'I must work the works of him that sent me, while it is day'—that means when he was alive— 'for the night cometh, when no man can work. As long as I am in the world, I am the light of the world.' Help the Master in his mission. The time for a spiritual revolution has come. It will arrive only when we lead a pure and chaste life. That will require some effort on our part. Have no fear; be true disciples of the Master and not of the mind; and then become a *Gurumukh* or mouthpiece of the Master . . . Do something now when the sun is shining; you won't be able to do anything after sunset. At present you are alive, and the Master is also in the physical body. Do not fritter away this opportunity."

These statements did seem ominous to us! I remember that the words, "The sun is about to set. Wake up before it is too late. You cannot depend on life," made a specially vivid impression on my mind, and I discussed the possible meaning of those words with other disciples. But we were totally unable to face up to the possible implications and so we left it. We could do nothing else.

In July 1973 the Master issued a circular letter asking His disciples not to write to Him anymore[8] and to discontinue sending Him their diaries. News of the circular spread like shock waves around the Western world, until it was published in *Sat Sandesh* where it could be read by all. Not to be

8. The circular is reprinted in *The Way of the Saints,* pp. 393-397.

able to write to the Master! A hard blow indeed. I felt very uneasy as it seemed to me that the reason for this had to be a deteriorating physical condition.

That September I went to India once again to sit at His feet. It was a beautiful three weeks. When I arrived He was up at Manav Kendra, the ideal community He was building near Dehra Dun. On one of the first nights I was pacing around and around the beautiful pool He had built there when I looked over and saw Him on the back porch of His house which was next to the pool. At first I thought He was asleep—He was sitting in a chair, unmoving—but looking closer I saw that He was in samadhi—He was radiating Light, and His face which in repose now looked older than old, had merged with that of His Master so that I was looking at both Their faces at once. It was an astounding sight and despite my years with Him, new to me: I had often seen Him turn totally into Baba Sawan Singh, but I had never seen Them co-exist in the same space before. I was very grateful to be granted this extraordinary privilege, and I gazed at Him for what seemed like many hours.

In February 1974, the Master held the gigantic World Conference on Unity of Man at the Ramlila Grounds in New Delhi. Many important religious and political leaders were present—Mrs. Gandhi addressed one of the sessions—and such well-known-in-America leaders as Yogi Bhajan and Pir Vilayat Khan were important participants. The Master used the occasion to issue a general invitation to His Western disciples to visit Him in India; about four hundred accepted, many many more by far than had ever gone to Sawan Ashram at one time before. I, however did not plan to go. I reasoned that I had just been there; that it was Judith's turn to go; and my one experience with a big spiritual conference in the past was not among my favorite

memories. No, this one was not for me. As various Satsangis from our area left to go, I kept not sending letters to
the Master explaining why I wasn't coming. Finally, when
my friends Tim and Sally Gallagher left, I really tried to
send a letter with them but I could not write it and I gave up.
A few days later I realized, just as I had in the motel room in
1972, that the Master wanted me and I had to go. So I went.
When I arrived, I learned that someone at the Ashram had
wanted to cable me in connection with a book I was
publishing, and had asked the Master if I was coming to the
Conference. "Coming?" asked the Master. "Of course
he's coming! He has to come. It's his job to be here." So I
had no choice.

The Conference was a big success, I guess; in many ways
it was tremendously inspiring, in other ways, not. In
retrospect, knowing that the Master's body was going to die
six months later, it seems almost that the Conference was an
excuse for getting as many of His children as possible to
come so that He could say goodbye. But that is not the
whole truth. In fact, He cared enormously about abstractions like "unity of man" and "universal love." No one
ever lived who did more to make those abstractions real in
His own life, and if all the participants at the Conference
did not share His total honesty and unbounded love for
human beings just because they were human beings, it was
not the Master's fault. He could take the rankest cliche
about love and/or service and make it as fresh and exciting
as if it had just been thought of, because He actually *lived*
those cliches and had *done* what the rest of us pay lip service
to. Consequently, the Conferences presided over by Him
cannot be discounted, even if they were ultimately disap-
pointing: if some of the politicians and religionists He was
compelled to work with had followed His example and lived

what they talked about so eloquently at the Conferences, it would have been another matter. The full potential of such gatherings would have been realized.

For me, the Conference at times was a real high: I participated in a panel on unity of religions with the Archbishop of Delhi, among others, and had to give a talk with no advance warning at all—none. I did it, and the result was one of the most exhilarating and satisfying senses of accomplishment I have ever felt. After the panel was over I was floating. I also addressed the whole Conference on one occasion: that was also a high, but less so than the panel. At other times, however, I felt tired, depressed, and ill, and it was with great effort that I went to the sessions at all.

The final day of the Conference was the Master's birthday and an early morning session (5:30 a.m.) was scheduled to celebrate it. While the Master said not a word in English during the whole session, it remains in my memory as the most powerful and charged Satsang I had ever attended. Master had never been more beautiful: sick, exhausted, eighty years old, He radiated love and easy good humor, deferred constantly to Yogi Bhajan (half His age), refused to give a proper discourse or to speak in English or to give out parshad—all of which was expected by various members of the audience. Instead, He conducted what looked like a good-humored private conversation (that just happened to go out over the microphone) with Yogi Bhajan and Pir Vilayat in Hindi, then asked the Yogi to translate for Him. At the end, rather than giving out parshad, He requested Yogi Bhajan to give it out, and Himself took the first parshad from the Yogi's hands. A gesture of humility that was astonishing under the circumstances: the tent, after all, contained fifty thousand persons who were disciples of Kirpal Singh, who were there to celebrate Kirpal

Singh's birthday, and who wanted Kirpal Singh's parshad. All in all, a very interesting morning.

After the Conference was over, and I had returned home, what stayed with me most strongly was gratitude for the personal grace that the Master had given me by allowing me to see Him privately so often when He was so terribly busy and there were so many others pressing on His time. Night after night I would find myself at His feet in His living-room, with a very few people or sometimes alone, with little or no effort on my part. On one occasion when I was sitting on the floor at His feet and we were alone, He said, out of a silence, "You should make the pond bigger." This was a surprise! I had to think very hard to remember that His last words to me as He was leaving Sant Bani Ashram in 1972 were, "Develop the pond more, please." He was referring to the pond which we had dug at the Ashram and which we were standing next to at that moment. Other people had also heard Him say that, and it had been recorded on tape: but because of the expense and difficulty involved in pumping the pond dry and getting the bulldozers in again, I had chosen to interpret His remarks as meaning that we should beautify the land around the pond and make it more suitable for meditation. In retrospect, it seems like a real cop-out on my part, but I had convinced myself that that was what He meant, and then forgotten about it. Now He was being very specific: "You should make the pond bigger." I stupidly asked, "You want us to make the pond bigger, Master?" He nodded. "Bigger—and deeper. Who knows? You might find a spring!" I promised Him that we would do it as soon as feasible and the following August, when He left the body, the work was just beginning; and while I was in India in connection with His passing, Judith wrote me that the bulldozer had uncovered a spring.

On another night, again we were alone, He looked deep into my eyes and said, "Thank God you have come!" That was all He said; the rest was silence, punctuated only by my weeping. (Of course, He was speaking from my point of view, not His. I didn't know, but He knew, that this was my last opportunity ever to have His physical darshan. We both knew how close I had been to not coming.)

On this night I had failed very badly. I had been feeling self-important, had lost my temper at a brother who didn't care for my advice, and had ignored some very specific instructions of the Master; in fact, I argued with Him about it. And He gave me only love back. As a consequence, after sitting in meditation all night I became very aware of what I had done and did my best to make everything right—not that we ever really can. But the point is that the Master is not a dictator. When we become disciples of a real Master we don't become slaves. He gently points out to us what would be for our own good. If we take it, fine; if we don't—well, He never says, "Bad person! You'll have to pay for this!" He leaves it up to us. It is because of the inherent dignity of the human being that He acts this way; as He has said, "I have come not to make you slaves, but to make you friends."

On the last day of my stay, which was also the last day I saw Him physically when He was wearing the body of Kirpal Singh, He again arranged it so that I saw Him in the morning for an hour or so. Present were Mr. Reno Sirrine, Bibi Hardevi, and me. He spoke about many things that were to be of great concern to either Reno or myself in the months ahead, and then He thanked me for keeping Sant Bani Ashram "straight" and not allowing His teachings to be mixed up with side issues. He said that the people who came there from the Sant Bani area used their time rightly, did not bother about secondary issues, did not complain about food or other things, but concentrated on meditation; and He appreciated it. I was very moved and did not know how to reply; later it seemed to me that very little of that was due to my doing, and that the dear brothers and sisters from the Sant Bani area were themselves responsible for having good sense.

That night I was feeling sad and depressed over leaving, even though He had given me another hour and had teased and joked with me and allowed me to sit there while people came and went. I did not feel the deep intense grief that I had felt in the past on leaving Him; felt instead a dull depression, like a toothache, and a feeling of wanting *more*. As we said goodbye to Him for the last time—about sixteen persons were leaving that night, including several group leaders—a friend and I were at the end of the line as we filed past Him at the door. When we reached Him, He put out His arm and stopped us from continuing and made us sit down again. He heaped parshad on us—bags and bags of sugar candy—and gave us the sweetest goodbye imaginable. When we got up to go, I felt happy and fulfilled and very very grateful. It was the last gift He gave me as Kirpal Singh.

Six months later, on August 21, 1974, we all received word that He had died. It was the end of our world as we had known it.

CHAPTER THREE

The Living Master:
His Mission and Technique

1. Confusion

Immediately upon learning of the Master's passing, I flew to India and, along with several other Western satsangis, arrived just in time to participate in the last portion of the cremation rites. It was terrible to be in India knowing that He had gone. The joy of my previous trips had turned inside out, and everything Indian that I had once loved now oppressed me. My grief was so deep as to be almost inexpressible: I cried often, and at odd times (it was not in my control either to cry or not to cry) but the tears were pitifully inadequate to express the vast emptiness; it deadened and made bitter everything I saw and heard. In the Sant Mat literature it is written in many places that a disciple should always pray to die before his Master does. It is true. It would have been much better.

The emptiness and bitterness were greatly compounded by what was going on around me. In my naivete, I had supposed that all His disciples felt the same way I did. Of course, the vast majority did. But within two days of my arrival it became only too obvious that some of the Master's so-called "important" disciples, that is, people who had been entrusted with positions of responsibility in carrying out Master's work, were maneuvering politically regarding a successor. I couldn't believe it. In retrospect, it is still hard to believe. But it happened.

143

I knew, of course, that there would probably be a successor. Intellectually, I welcomed it. What would seekers do if there was no Master? Surely, in the light of what I knew about Sant Mat, and of my own experience, to leave the world without a Master would be the cruellest joke yet. But emotionally, I was unable to cope with the idea of giving my devotion to "somebody else," which is how I saw it. I was unable to look past the emptiness and devastation of my Master's leaving, and talk of a successor struck me on a gut level as being in the worst possible taste.

But worse yet were the political maneuverings. I use the term advisedly; there is no other way to describe them. Because I was the editor of the English-language monthly magazine, and therefore considered to be in a "position of influence," I was more aware of these maneuverings than many of the Western disciples present. I was expected to "throw my support" for a certain "candidate" for Mastership, exactly as if he were running for the U.S. Congress. My response was anger—much too much anger, as it caused me to forget an essential part of my Master's teaching—and nausea. I was completely unable to see in any "candidate" the same Power which I had responded to in my Master, and still less was I able to after learning that there was supposed to be a will, drawn up and executed by the Master, which named someone as the Master's successor.

As it happened, this will was never found. But that it was seriously brought forth as a criterion was astonishing, because if there was one criterion of the successor that Kirpal Singh had emphasized was totally invalid, it was the possession of a will. Time and again throughout his life, he had stressed that spirituality was not transmitted via written documents; so much did he stress it that to many of us it seemed to follow that the claiming of such a document was in itself sufficient reason to not take the claimant seriously. And why should Kirpal Singh not stress this? He himself had been forcibly ejected from his Master's ashram in Beas because of the existence of a document naming someone else as successor; while he never in any way reacted or objected to this, and pursued his spiritual mission from scratch (since the overwhelming majority of his Master's disciples preferred to believe the document), it was unthinkable that he should have chosen such a means to have named his successor.

Besides, one of the criteria in determining who might or might not be a Master was that he/she had risen above the demands of the ego. If therefore someone both actively wanted the position and demonstrated hurt and bitterness at having it denied to him (both of which I saw with my own eyes), at the very least it showed a terrible misunderstanding on his part as to what it was he was striving for. When Kirpal Singh, despite having been given orders by Baba Sawan Singh to carry on the work, was told to leave the Dera (as Sawan Singh's ashram was called) he left—abandoning, in the process, a house he had built and paid for himself—and went into the Himalayas, where he spent five months in full-time meditation. It was only in response to orders from his Master within, together with the pleas of the few fellow-disciples who recognized his stature, that he came back into the world and began actively functioning as a Master. Even then, he made no effort to disturb the people at Beas but began his own ashram in Delhi, hundreds of miles away; and to my knowledge, he never referred to anyone at Beas in any terms other than love.

For the interesting fact is that in the history of Sant Mat, this is the norm: that the succession is disputed after the passing of the Master. It could be taken, I suppose as a sign that ultimately the Masters have failed: they teach love and humility after all, and what happens during these times is anything but that. But this is really a false criterion, that turns the Masters' forgiveness and compassion against them: it is because they respond to the needs of others and initiate anyone who really wants it that they lay themselves open to charges of having failed because their disciples are unworthy. To be fair, each individual would have to be carefully examined on the basis of where he was at the time he was initiated and how far he has come since.

The Masters themselves are aware of all this. Baba Sawan Singh wrote, "A Saint is lucky if he gets one or two genuine seekers during his whole lifetime." Kirpal Singh wrote, "No Master has ever been interested in attracting large numbers to himself and quantity has never been my aim. It is quality that counts and I would rather have a handful of disciples, nay even one, who can sacrifice his ego on the spiritual altar and learn to live by love, than millions who understand not the value and meaning of these virtues." But still they initiate, as a general rule, anyone who comes to them, and all Masters have said that the true criterion is whether or not the prospective initiate really *wants* it.

No, considering the enormity of what the Masters are trying to do, and the weight of the odds against them, it is no reflection on them if the majority of their disciples forget everything when their Master departs—just as it is natural for children to tear a classroom apart when the teacher leaves the room. What really is at stake is whether or not they can take *anybody* all the way—whether or not they can make *somebody* what they themselves are. If they cannot do that much, we might be justified in saying they have failed. But so far, all Masters have been able to do that; and

Swami Ji's statement, "The Satguru is an incarnation eternally existent upon the earth," remains true. A world without a living Master would be hell indeed.

Before I left India in September 1974, the mass of Kirpal Singh's disciples had divided into two factions, one centered around a candidate for Mastership, the other around the possession of Sawan Ashram. Because of my fierce opposition to the person put forth as a Master, I, to my eternal shame, identified myself with the second faction and said and published many things which I bitterly regretted afterward. Although I do not feel that all my initial perceptions were wrong, I came to see the basic truth of the idea of non-violence: that to oppose something is to give it strength. As time went on whatever moral difference had existed between the factions eroded until one of them (it was impossible to find out which, because both maintained the other had started it) brought suit against the other in a court of law—over possession of the Ashram!—and the other fought back!—the final blackening of Kirpal Singh's name.

But behind this overwhelming crashing of competing chords was playing the sweet and harmonious song of Ajaib—at first so softly that none of us could hear it, but eventually it became so loud that it drowned out all the rest.

I first heard of Ajaib Singh shortly after I returned from India. A friend of mine, also present at Sawan Ashram during those difficult days, had heard of him at the Ashram and had gone to see him. He found him in a remote village in the Rajasthan desert, overwhelmed with grief at the Master's passing. He liked him and was impressed by him, although he had no idea as to whether he was the new Master or not. He added that he was almost a legend at Sawan Ashram (although very few knew his name)—a guru from Rajasthan who had been initiated together with his entire following. (Actually, at this time Ajaib Singh had not been functioning as a guru at all. He had never initiated anyone, and he had never really had any disciples in the strict sense. But he had a wide and growing reputation as an authentic holy man, and many people no doubt considered themselves to be his disciples.)

My friend said that Ajaib Singh specifically stated that he did not wish to be a guru, and that he was leaving for the wilderness shortly. He added that he had previously heard prophecies to the effect that the next Master would be simpler and less educated than Kirpal Singh, and that he would appear in Rajasthan.

I was impressed—enough to publish a brief account of the meeting with Ajaib Singh in *Sat Sandesh*. It all rang true to me, and the name "Ajaib" produced the same internal reaction as the name "Kirpal" had seventeen years before. But beyond that, I didn't know; he was in the wilderness, so I guessed we would have to wait until he came out.

In June 1975 a record low-point was reached: one of the factions struggling for physical possession of Sawan Ashram published a book supposedly heralding the advent of a new Master. In fact, however, the book was a cruel examination of a sister disciple to whom Kirpal Singh had shown much favor. As I read the first few pages and realized what it was all about, I felt as though I had been shot. I began to tremble and grew sick with fear: how far, how very very far we had gone from the path of love shown to us by our Master! Was there any hope for us? No wonder the Master in His new coat had not shown up yet. Why would any Master care two cents about such a collection of so-called "disciples," who obviously had no more comprehension of the meaning of His life and teachings than a baboon does of ours?

Yet he did care. Even as I despaired, the first intimation of the Master's coming came in the form of a letter from a Colombian radiologist, a distinguished and respected initiate of Kirpal Singh, then in his fifties, who told his daughter and son-in-law (both good friends of mine, who lived near the Ashram) that the Master Kirpal had told him within that Ajaib Singh was almost ready to come forth.

Then, about the time of Kirpal Singh's birthday (February 6) 1976, the Master ordered me, from within, to go to Rajasthan and find Ajaib Singh. I did not want to go. I was afraid. But no appeal was possible and no peace did I have until I had bought my ticket.

2. The Road to Rajasthan

On the plane over I got scared again. My whole trip seemed presumptuous and arrogant beyond measure—as several fellow disciples had told me, trying to dissuade me from going. What did I think I was going to accomplish? Mournfully, I reflected that I had no special competence in regard to assessing the qualifications of Saints. Even if I physically located him—which seemed more unlikely the more I thought about it—how on earth was *I* going to know whether he was a Master or not? I had been able to recognize Kirpal Singh because He had been my own Guru Who had spoken to my soul. Would it be the same with Ajaib Singh? Suppose it wasn't? What would I do then? Then I remembered the parting words of a dear sister at Sant Bani Ashram: she had reminded me that Master Kirpal had said in the last days of His life when someone had asked Him how they would recognize His successor, "Well, look here: If your friend comes with a different coat on, won't you recognize him?" Susan had said, "If you keep that in mind, you can't go wrong." Now remembering her words, I felt comforted: she was right. If I kept in mind that I was looking for my friend in a new coat, then how could I go wrong? As long as I didn't settle for less.

On arrival in Delhi I visited Sawan Ashram, met the brother who had recently been installed as guru there, and made arrangements with my friends Kulwant and Linda Bagga to go to Rajasthan with them— Kulwant to act as interpreter. For various reasons it was a week before we could go, and I spent that week with Kulwant's family.

That week at the Bagga home remains one of the happiest I have ever experienced. The Baggas could be called, I suppose, a typical Indian family—father, mother, paternal grandmother, six children, plus Kulwant and Linda—all living in a three-room apartment. Obviously my presence aggravated the overcrowding, but it didn't matter: I was treated like a visiting prince the whole time I was there and made to feel that the family would be infinitely saddened were I to leave.

The afternoon before we were to leave we purchased bus tickets for Ganga Nagar. We had planned to go by first-class train, but we discovered that bus tickets were much cheaper and, since the bus left at 5 a.m. and the train at 10 p.m. we could save a whole day. We were also told that the train took thirteen hours and the bus seven—which meant that we could theoretically be in Ajaib Singh's village—assuming that he was there, which no one knew for sure—that afternoon. It sounded good.

The next morning before dawn the three of us, our only luggage my sleeping bag which we had filled with everything we thought we might need and a gigantic bag of food lovingly prepared by Kulwant's mother and sisters, took a taxi to the bus station. It was pitch dark and the station appeared to be a yard with buses scattered at random all over it, pointing every which way and with no visible indication at all as to where they were going. Nonetheless Kulwant led us straight to our bus, although it was a long walk to the farthest point of the yard.

The bus was an average Indian bus, with hard wooden seats set closer together than American legs appreciate: Indians are, on the average, smaller than Americans, and the buses reflect this. Nevertheless, despite the discomfort and the uncertainty surrounding the end of the journey a wave of complete and wonderful happiness came over me; I felt unmistakably the Master's presence and I *knew* everything was happening the way it was supposed to be. As the bus pulled out of the yard, I flattened my face to the window and stared out at the pitch-dark Indian countryside I loved so well. Softly I began to sing a song written by my friend David Teed—or maybe I should say the song began to sing me, because I couldn't help it:

> *At the sweet ambrosial hour*
> *Bhajan and Simran do—*
> *Keep your mind in sweet remembrance*
> *Kirpal Singh loves you.*

Over and over went the song as the bus rolled along and streaks of grey began to appear in the blackness. Never had "the sweet ambrosial hour" (*amrit vela*: the three hours before dawn) seemed sweeter or more ambrosial—never had I been more aware that Kirpal Singh did indeed love me. On and on went the bus and my happiness, based on an acute sense that I was doing what I was meant to do and that I was right to be just where I was, grew with every mile.

But as the daylight displaced the dark and the bus began to grow hot and crowded, as the road grew bumpier and bumpier (or so it seemed) and the seat grew harder and the leg space smaller, I began to wish heartily that we were at our destination. At every stop, more people crowded on; at every stop Linda, who was feeling very ill, had to leave the bus, accompanied by Kulwant, to relieve herself. This meant that I had to guard their seats—the bench directly behind mine—and since I didn't speak Hindi, the only way I could do it was to lean across their seat and bodily prevent anyone from sitting there—without explanation.

The hours went on. At noontime I said to Kulwant, "Are we there yet? It's been seven hours." He said, "No, we're not there yet. I don't think we're very near either." At one o'clock I asked the same question and got the same answer. At two o'clock—at three o'clock—at five o'clock he said, "Well, I don't think it's far now." I looked out the window and saw that the landscape had certainly changed. Instead of the flat plain that is typical of the area surrounding Delhi we were now riding through the desert—in places just rolling waves of white sand, other places irrigated patches of green growth. Sometimes the irrigated plots ended abruptly in the sand, so that they made neat squares that looked as though they had been laid there by a giant hand. I saw camels, too—many of them, and for the first time in my life I saw a camel harnessed to a plow, like a horse. I was fascinated by the desert, and it was clear we were indeed in Rajasthan— the desert state of India, historic home of the Rajput warriors and many saints, and also very near the site of one of the oldest civilizations so far known—the Indus Valley culture, some of whose cities were only a few miles from our destination. The water in the canals that were constantly visible, and which made the green acres possible, came ultimately from the Indus River.

Kulwant was right—it wasn't far now. Another hour

went by, during which the constant bouncing on the hard wooden seat and the permanence of my squeezed-up position turned my body into one long rack of pain: it was now twelve hours since we had started (on a journey supposed to take seven), my kidneys felt like they were down in my left foot, I could not remember a time when they didn't feel like that, and it went on and on and on and on—bounce, bump, clunk, uhh, bounce, bump, clunk, uhh—until finally, incredibly, we pulled into a large dusty yard somewhere and Kulwant said, "We're here." What was left of us got up, went out, and looked around. It seemed to us as though we were a million miles from Nowhere. What now? Kulwant and Linda looked to me. I recalled our meager directions. "Well—we're supposed to find the first apothecary shop on the right after we leave the railroad station. Of course— we're not at the railroad station. So I guess the first thing is to find the railroad station." The logic of this seemed irrefutable. We looked around for a taxi, but there weren't any; there were no cars at all anywhere in sight. What there were, in abundance, was bicycle rickshas, and an eager young man pedaled up on his and requested our business.

Now, I don't like bicycle rickshas as a matter of principle; I doubt that most Americans do. Sitting in a carriage while another human being pedals me strikes me as particularly reprehensible, and I ride in them as little as possible. I have heard, and I see no reason to doubt it, that the average bicycle ricksha driver does not live past fifty. The strain is inhuman. On the other hand, I am reasonably certain that most of them don't think of it that way. To them, it's their livelihood, and my refusal to ride with them means that much less food on the table that night. Whether it is better to die at 50 from overwork or at 30 from starvation is perhaps unanswerable; it is the kind of question that the vast majority of persons who have ever lived have been faced with. It is the essence of life, lived only in terms of the physical plane.

Anyway, this particular driver wanted our business so badly that he assured us that he could take all three of us at once, plus our luggage. We were dubious, but he was persuasive, so we all climbed in and he started off for the railway station. We had not reached the road, however, when his bicycle chain broke, presumably from the strain. He became very sad and we felt sorry for him. We paid him something—less certainly than the fare he would have received for the whole trip—and climbed into *two* rickshas that had pulled up beside us. This time we made it.

Out on the street, it became obvious that we were in a different world than Delhi—almost as different as Delhi was from the United States. For one thing, there were not only no taxis, there were few cars at all—none. We saw a few trucks, buses, and an occasional jeep, but that was all. The streets, which were crowded with motor traffic in Delhi, were here crowded with bicycles—and camels. I had not realized the extent to which the camel is still utilized in the modern world. I had seen a camel or two from time to time in other parts of India, but never anything like this: wherever we looked we saw camels, tied to posts on the side of the street, pulling carts, carrying people. And there were thousands of bicycles.

The natural result of the absence of motor traffic was the purity of the air and silence. Delhi is suffering from an advanced case of acute air pollution—at times it is almost impossible for someone not used to the air to breathe without getting sick—and from an equally advanced case of ear pollution. It is astonishingly noisy. A great deal of the noise is traceable directly to the automobile. So is most of the air pollution. In Ganga Nagar there was neither, and the thought crossed my mind that this was really a very pleasant city to be in.

In a short while we arrived at the railroad station, and I directed the drivers to take us in and then come out again (as though we had just gotten off a train), making sure we turned to the right as we came out. As we did, Kulwant yelled across to me, "Look at the apothecary shops!" It was true. A casual glance revealed the abnormal number of them. What to do? I yelled back, "Well, we'll still have to go to the first one on the right." We were already there, so Kulwant went in while Linda and I—each in our rickshas—waited outside. People began to gather round. Kulwant came out. "They've never heard of Dogar Mal." (The man who was to be our guide to Ajaib Singh.) My heart sank, but somehow I had been expecting it. "Well, we'll just have to try the others." Kulwant nodded valiantly, and went on to the next one. Meanwhile the crowd around our rickshas was growing larger. It was silent and respectful, but *large*—and increasing rapidly. Over the heads of the crowd I could see Kulwant going from one apothecary shop to another. Something clicked in my mind, and I yelled to Linda, "Let's forget it for tonight. If we can find a hotel somewhere, we'll get some rest and try again in the morning." In my heart I said, "Well, Master, we've done our best; we're here, now it's up to You." At that moment Kulwant returned to say that he had been to a dozen apothecary shops and none of them had ever heard of Dogar Mal. I started to tell him to forget it and we would try to find a hotel when a portly, well-dressed man pushed his way through the crowd (which by now was mammoth, it seemed—I could no longer see where it ended) and asked in English what we wanted. I told him we were looking for a man named Dogar Mal, and he said, his eyes lighting up, "I know him! He's a Radhasoami!" I said, not quite believing it, "That's right." He thought a moment and said, "He is not here just now, but his relative—his family man—is nearby. I will just fetch him." He was gone; within two minutes a pleasant, balding, youngish man appeared in front of my ricksha and said, smiling, "You're an initiate of Kirpal Singh!" I said, "Yes!" He said, smiling broadly, "So am I! Come on!" and led us to an apothecary shop nearby—he was Dogar Mal's cousin, and his shop was the one we were supposed to find, although it was definitely not the first one on the right after the railroad station.

Mr. Arora—which was our new friend's name—led us into his shop, seated us on comfortable chairs, served us tea, and sent a messenger to bring his cousin. He and the portly gentleman whose kindness had made our rescue possible sat with us, and Mr. Arora said to me, "You are the editor of *Sat Sandesh*." I was stunned—to have come all this distance, gone through all the discomfort of the bus ride and the turmoil and the strangeness and uncertainty of the crowd and the street outside and then to be *recognized* —it was too good to be true. I exulted in the supreme peace and comfort of that moment and replied, "How on earth do you know that?" He said that he had attended the Unity of Man Conference in Delhi two years before and had heard me give a talk. I was amazed and grateful.

In a few minutes the messenger was back—on a motor scooter—with Dogar Mal, a gentle old man with a big white moustache, riding on the back. I explained to him that I had been given his name, and that we wanted very much to see Ajaib Singh. Dogar Mal was silent for a few minutes, then he said, "Well, I took your friend to see Sant Ajaib Singh; but after that Sant Ji told me specifically not to give his address to anyone or bring anyone to see him.''

Silence. His statement floated out into the middle of the room and hung there. Part of my mind gave up and surrendered to Master—again—and another part began working furiously. In the meantime Linda said desperately, "Does he know that Russell has come all the way from America just to see Ajaib Singh?" I said, "No, no, that's all right, I'm thinking," and I had just about made up my mind to invoke the authority of the Master within—I was praying, "Master, this can't be the end of the road, it can't be"—when Dogar Mal cleared his throat and said, "Well, it's too late to go this afternoon; we'll have a jeep here by 9:30 tomorrow morning." Whew! We thanked him profusely, and Mr. Arora invited us to spend the night in his house, which we did most comfortably and gratefully. He and his wife entertained us beautifully.

The following morning Dogar Mal was there with the jeep. He explained that he couldn't accompany us all the way, but that the jeep would stop in Padampur, the next village, and Sardar Jagir Singh, who knew the way, would join us. Before he left us, Kulwant asked him what his opinion of Ajaib Singh was. He replied, "In my opinion, he is a *Sant*, definitely; but he doesn't want to be a guru, that is certain."

I asked him if Ajaib Singh would be glad to see us (a legitimate question, I felt, in light of what he had told us the day before) and he said "Oh yes, he'll be glad to see you. But he doesn't want to be a guru." Kulwant said as Dogar Mal left us, "I think this visit will be very interesting." It turned out that Ajaib Singh *was* at the village of Satatararbi, where he had been last seen, and that was where we were now headed.

But first we stopped at Padampur. At the time I wished

we hadn't; now it seems somehow appropriate—one final hurdle to be overcome. For S. Jagir Singh did his very best to discourage us and prevent us from going. We all became depressed, and I asked Kulwant if it was really necessary for him to accompany us; he said that Jagir Singh was not coming, but that he was sending his son.[1] As soon as possible, we were in the jeep and back on the road.

At first our spirits were low and the aftertaste of Jagir Singh's conversation hung on. But as we went on, the sheer adventure of what we were doing again affected us, and our spirits lifted. I said to Linda, "Well the next hour or so will tell the tale: it will either be the biggest downer in the history of mankind or we will have found something." She agreed. I asked her how she was feeling, and she said that she was feeling fine—that her illness had gone away when the jeep ride started.

By this time we were off the tar road (it had ended in Padampur) and were literally driving across the desert. Later I tried to explain this by saying "there were roads that aren't roads." This was true: the "road" was a track scratched in the sand, and at many points it disappeared; at these points, the driver would get out, look all around, walk a number of feet in every direction, finally decide what way he wanted, and then we would go that way. Wherever possible, he would ask directions, but usually it was not possible because there was no one to ask. One time at a crossroads in the midst of mustard fields, two men on a camel came riding by—they were staring at us and this time we stared right back. It was fascinating to watch them. Our driver asked directions of them also, and they pointed up the correct road.

1. Jagir Singh, who has since died, later apologized publicly to Sant Ajaib Singh at the monthly Satsang for this incident, humbly asking the forgiveness of the entire Sangat.

Reflecting on this ride afterward, and searching for words to convey it to others, I realized that this was "the wilderness" in the Biblical sense. It was in this sort of country that the Essenes had their community, that both the prophet Elijah and John the Baptist (the same person, according to the Bible) sojourned for many years, that the Desert Fathers made their caves. Thousands of years of spiritual accomplishment rose up and surrounded me as we drove along, mostly through sand, occasionally through irrigated fields or down the middle of tiny villages, and sometimes— most wonderful of all—along the banks of an irrigation canal, alive with green trees and bushes and many-colored tropical birds. Other images confronted me also: hundreds of fairy tales and stories—the hills outside the castle in *The Princess and the Goblin,* the Land of Ev in the Oz books, and, most potent of all, the Waste Land outside the Grail castle—and the thought came that it was absolutely right and proper for the Master to live in the middle of the wilderness. Except for us and our jeep, the world we were in was essentially unchanged from Bible times; we were all that would have been out of place two thousand years ago.

Finally, after a two-hour journey through time and space, the jeep pulled into a little village. Lots of excited talk and gestures pointing back the way we had come; then the jeep turned around, went back maybe a quarter of a mile, and stopped in front of a mud wall with a wooden double gate set in the middle of it. The driver honked his horn, and the gates slowly opened and the jeep drove into a spacious courtyard adjoining a large building again made of hard-baked mud. There were a few people around—not many—and they greeted us warmly and politely, although they did not act in any way surprised to see us. We were ushered through a low-ceilinged room into a small inner court-yard where a table and chairs were brought, and within a very few minutes the man we had come so far to see came through a door and greeted us.

I was excited, but I did my best to maintain my objectivity. I remembered again what Susan had said to me just before I left home: that Kirpal Singh had said, "if a friend comes in a new coat, won't you recognize him?," and if I kept that in mind I would not make any mistakes. I looked at him carefully and I saw a vigorous middle-aged Sikh, not nearly as tall as Kirpal Singh (who had been unusually tall for an Indian), approximately the same color skin (coffee-brown) as Kirpal Singh, dressed very simply in brown Punjabi-style trousers and a dark brown threadbare sweater, and, in the beginning, wrapped in a blanket in typical Indian style. He greeted us politely. Kulwant introduced us to him, he sat down with us and smiled at me. When he smiled, he was Kirpal Singh. It took me a few minutes to realize it, and then I understood—it was Kirpal Singh sitting there, smiling at me! The more I looked into his eyes, the clearer it became: they were definitely the eyes of Kirpal Singh, and they were looking at me like an old friend: "Hello, how are you? What took you so long?" My mind shot back to that night in Virginia in 1972 when Master had smiled at me and asked me, "Were you lost?" I saw that same face with those same eyes sitting three feet away across the table, ten thousand miles from nowhere in the middle of the desert, smiling at me with recognition, with joy, and with such love that my heart melted, my eyes filled with tears, and that overwhelming joy that I had always felt in my Master's presence and that I had thought I would never feel again welled up and I knew with complete and absolute assurance that my Friend was with me in His new coat and that I was sitting in my Master's presence. In my heart I was shouting, "Hello, Master, thank You, thank You."

In my heart, I say, because all that I was describing was happening on one level, while something seemingly very different was going on outside. I could not tell whether Sant Ajaib Singh was sure of who I was on the outer level or not. Not that I expected him to—I knew that he did not read English, had never been to Sawan Ashram in Delhi during Master's lifetime, and probably had never heard of *Sat Sandesh* or Sant Bani Ashram. Why should he? But my name rang some sort of bell, because within five minutes of our meeting he was rebuking me for the part I had played in the controversy among the disciples after Kirpal Singh's death. Here was something original. Other brothers who were considered to be gurus had praised me to the skies—one of them right after Master's leaving, the other in Sawan Ashram just a few days before, when he told me I had done splendid work bearing witness to the truth. Ajaib Singh had a different idea. He said, with a big Kirpal Singh smile,[2] "I was very surprised to see the letter that Russell wrote." His words filled me with foreboding, but his eyes—my Master's eyes—were dancing, and he was smiling—my Master's smile. My heart sank, exactly as it used to when Master was rebuking me (I knew what he was referring to—a particularly strong letter, tearing one of the gurus in whom I did not believe apart, had been translated into Hindi and circulated in India) and I said, "Why?" And he said—still smiling, his eyes dancing—"Because it had nothing to do with Sant Mat." I knew with my whole being that my Master was telling me something which I would ignore at my soul's peril. I looked into His face and there was

2. Under ordinary circumstances, Ajaib Singh's smile is very different from Kirpal Singh's.

Master there—totally loving, eyes dancing, smiling at me, and He was rebuking me—*just* the way Master used to rebuke me! I said, "I was wrong." And He smiled—He accepted it.

He was not happy at all about having had his name published as an alternative Master and having been set up in opposition to anybody. He said that he had respect for all of them—"Why should I have been dragged into this?" It was clear that Dogar Mal's assessment had been correct—he had no desire to be a guru, and certainly he was not going to fight anybody over it. He mentioned the lawsuit over Sawan Ashram with great sadness, and said that anything would be better than that—no matter who started it.

He told me also that the management at Sawan Ashram had telegraphed him in December to come to Delhi—presumably to be checked out and, if he passed, offered the *gaddi* (or seat of honor) there. But he wouldn't go; and as he told me about it he laughed gleefully and said, "Who wants to be a guru? What is there in being a guru, tell me that? Is it not better to be a disciple?"

He confirmed that Master Kirpal had given him the authority to initiate but he said that he was hiding, and that he could not come out until things had changed among the satsangis. I digested this and weighed the facts of the matter: here he was, surrounded by a few hundred people who loved him and took him seriously and had (as I found out later) built the present ashram for him without even knowing for sure whether he would actually live there or not—"We built it only on hope"—he had ample time for meditation, his livelihood was provided by managing the farm adjoining the ashram, he was completely free from the burden of carrying thousands of disciples who had no intention of taking him seriously—why should he not hide? Then I thought of it another way: here the Master Power—the essence of Kirpal Singh—had reincarnated into the physical world, and the mass of disciples were too busy fighting each other to care! A few hundred villagers in the Rajasthan desert had Him all to themselves! It seemed a perfect cosmic joke.

He gave me no guarantees about the future, as to whether he would initiate Westerners or take on any mission in the west; in fact, he said that he was going to go into full-time meditation for a year, beginning in a month. My heart sank but I asked him for one final concession: Would he turn anyone away who came to see him? He said compassionately that he would turn no one away, that anyone who came looking for truth was welcome. Previously he had confirmed that he had indeed told Dogar Mal not to bring anyone to see him, so I asked him if he was sorry we had come. He said with great humor, his eyes dancing, "No! I am very happy when anyone who wants to know the truth comes."

As the afternoon wore on, a meal was brought and we left the courtyard for an adjoining room where we sat at a table and ate. Ajaib Singh personally served us with his own hands and sat with us, although he did not eat anything. As we talked more, a feeling of contentment and light-heartedness came over us and a lot of laughter was happening—sweet laughter, as I had not known it since the passing of my Master. A sizable number of disciples had gathered in the courtyard and were listening intently to every word. At one point, Ajaib Singh mentioned that when Master gave him the commission to give Naam, He had told him not to hide it. There was an obvious question here, and I took a deep breath and asked, wondering what the reaction would be, "Well, if Master told you not to hide it, why are you hiding?'' There was a tremendous roar of laughter from everywhere—all the disciples were laughing—but most of it came from him, who laughed with a glee and abandon that were beautiful to see. When he finished he said humbly that he was hiding only on a temporary basis; that when the fighting among the disciples died down, if anyone wanted him to, he would come out.

Before eating he had left us for a few minutes to wash up, relieve ourselves, etc. (His personal latrine, which he offered to us for our own use, was a deep hole in the ground, dug in a cubicle in the courtyard, over which one squatted; a bucket of water was brought to us for our bathing) and we quickly compared notes. I said, ''I don't know about you two, but I'm with him!'' We talked fast and excitedly and the three of us agreed that the *least* we could say was that he was a very holy man and we loved him.

As the meal ended, it came to me very strongly from within that the time had come to go back—that we had got what we came for. We took our leave accordingly, and Ajaib Singh lovingly came out to the jeep and said goodbye to us. Linda was crying, and he patted her on her head consolingly and said, ''You are my dear daughter.''

The ride back to Ganga Nagar was long, cold and dark and we arrived at the Aroras' well into the evening. They graciously agreed to put us up for another night and curiously asked us what we thought of him. When we told them that we liked him, they revealed to us things that they had previously not told us: that they had been initiated at the same time he was, in 1967, only he had been initiated in a separate room; that whenever Master had visited Ganga Nagar He had kept Ajaib Singh by His side constantly, including on the dais when He held Satsang; and that after Master's passing, the Ganga Nagar satsangis had invited

Ajaib Singh to hold Satsang for them. The Aroras said that he had done so twice with beauty and power, very much as Master had done; but intense pressure from one of the factions that had emerged after Master left had made things very difficult for the satsangis, and when Ajaib Singh learned of it he declined to come anymore.

The Aroras also told us that Master habitually referred to Ajaib Singh as "Sant Ji," that is, "my beloved saint," and that this was how he was commonly referred to by the people of the area also.

Linda's illness, which had lifted for the entire time in Sant Ji's ashram, had returned as the jeep left the area, and by the time we reached Ganga Nagar she was very sick; she spent a miserable night, and Kulwant and I realized that she could not take a bus trip back. The next morning, on the advice of our friends, we purchased three first-class train tickets, and at 6 p.m. that day (February 25) left for Delhi. For the first part of our ride we had a compartment to ourselves, although it had four berths, and we peacefully rode along. I felt, as I looked out the window, a real sense of gratitude and thanks to the Master Who had brought me to the completion of the task which He had given me. I did not know what Sant Ji was going to do, and on one level I was taking back little enough for the dear ones at home; but my heart was at peace because I knew where the Master was on the physical plane and because the incredible ineffable joy of those hours in Kirpal Singh's presence—of His dancing loving laughing eyes and the touching of my soul with His—had not left me and in fact never did leave me.

Later that night, around midnight, Linda was sound asleep and I was dozing when a fearful knocking arose at our door. Kulwant told it to go away, but at last the knocker convinced him that he was the fourth legitimate member of our compartment. (In India people are always trying to gain entry into first-class compartments, and will say or do anything in order to bring it about.) After the man entered, they talked for a long time (for some reason partly in English) and I was able to follow the gist of the conversation. Kulwant was explaining to him where we had been and why and pointing at me, explained that I had organized the trip to Rajasthan. Abandoning all efforts to sleep, I joined the conversation and the man (a distinguished, tall, middle-aged Indian businessman) asked me if I was searching for a Guru for myself. I said, "No, not exactly; I have a Guru but He has left the body, and we went to see if this Saint might not be His successor." He asked me my Guru's name and when I told him, "Kirpal Singh," he became wildly excited —jumping up, he began dancing around the little compartment, shouting, "I can't believe it!: He was my Guru too! I'm his disciple too! I can't believe it!" and indeed it was easier to believe that this meeting in the middle of the night on a train plowing through the Indian countryside was planned and purposeful than it was to believe that it was an accident, so high were the odds against it.

He insisted on buying us tea at the next stop and then asked us about our trip to Rajasthan and what we had found there. We told him what we felt and he was very interested. Then he asked me what I thought of the factionalism and fighting among the disciples in Delhi. I started to answer in a usual way, but as I opened my mouth Sant Ji's words came into them and I said, quoting him exactly, that I had respect for all the people involved—they were all dear to my Master. That pleased him enormously, and a beautiful night was passed very quickly as we all became lost in the sweet remembrance of our Master in that unlikeliest of settings. As Linda said afterward, the incident showed us that if Master had given us a message to give, He would also send people to receive it.

We arrived in Delhi at 6 a.m. and finally made it to the Baggas' apartment about 7. After a few hours sleep (for me—Kulwant spent the time telling his family what had happened) Kulwant and I went downtown where I arranged a flight home for that night. I felt that what I was supposed to do had been done and I wanted to get home as quickly as possible. After confirming the flight, we stopped at the post office to send a cable telling Judith and the Ashramites when I was coming. The cable began, HAVE FOUND AJAIB SINGH AND HE IS REAL WE LOVE HIM . . . Later I learned that there was dancing in the Ashram when it arrived.

I returned home, exhausted and stretched, to the most eager and responsive audience a weary traveler could hope for. I had been back only a few hours when someone told me she also wanted to make the trip; then another; then another; and so it went. I was apprehensive, because Sant Ji had told me he was going back into full-time meditation, and I was not sure I wanted to be responsible for an army of uninvited seekers descending on the seemingly fragile ashram. I need not have worried. On the day he had fixed for going back into meditation he was then giving darshan to the first group of disciples; another group followed, and another, in a string that has continued to this day. Sant Ji once said, in connection with the possibility of his coming to America, "The pullers have to pull and the Sender send." This has been true of all Masters: that the orders of God within have to find expression through the love of those who care. "When the disciples are ready the Guru appears." The Sender may send, but if the pullers aren't pulling, who will receive what is being sent?

These early groups were intensely curious about Sant Ji's

early life, and in response to their questiong he revealed that
he had been born on September 11, 1926; that his search for
God had involved many different gurus and yogic practices,
including the famous *panch agni tap*, or "austerity of the
five fires"; that he spent ten years with a sadhu named Baba
Bishan Das, who eventually initiated him into the first two
inner planes of Surat Shabd Yoga just before leaving the
body; that he had spent considerable time in the Army and
apart from that he had earned his living as a farmer; and
that he had refused either to marry or to inherit his father's
property which he arranged to pass on to an illegitimate un-
touchable boy in his native village. Eventually he settled at
Kunichuk in Rajasthan, where he built an ashram, acquired
a large following, and waited for the Master Whom Bishan
Das had prophesied would come to him and give him the
rest of the initiation. In the year 1966 he began seeing the
Radiant Form of Swami Ji Maharaj, a past Master, in his
meditations, and that Form gradually changed into
another, Whom he did not recognize, but Who remained
with him for a year or so—until Kirpal Singh came to Rajasthan in 1967 and Sant Ji recognized the Radiant One
Who had been blessing his meditations.

Eventually Sant Ji sent word to me to return, as it was time
to begin the work of world-wide initiation. He had initiated
seekers from his own area in Rajasthan, but up till now no
one else. In response to his request, I did go back in May
1976, this time accompanied by Judith, our son Eric, and
several others, including two seekers wanting initiation. We
stayed eleven days with him, and I agreed to serve him as his
American Representative with all my heart and soul, recognizing that it was my Master Kirpal Whom I was serving in
fact; and he did initiate the two candidates, authorizing me at
the same time to initiate on his behalf elsewhere in the world.

That initiation represented the final open door in the long passageway to my Master's Feet. I have told of the various ways in which my Master had shown me that He was indeed wearing this new coat. But up till now this had not been solidly and unmistakeably confirmed in my meditations. I had had glimpses within of Sant Ji's beauty and His oneness with Kirpal, but they had been only glimpses; and that had troubled me a little bit, mostly because of the taunts of others. I knew from the inside out that my destiny lay with Sant Ji, and knew that to serve Him was to serve my Master; but there was so much controversy and bitterness in those days, and people were talking so loudly about never doing a thing without having it confirmed a hundred times over in meditation, that it worried me that my very strong experiences on the outer had been backed up by glimpses only on the inner. Nevertheless, I agreed to work for Him and to initiate for Him because I loved Him and because the voice of my Master, which was the voice of my soul, was telling me with every breath to do it. But that first westerner-initiation changed everything; I received the confirmation that everyone said I ought to have a hundred times over, stronger than I would have presumed to ask for under any circumstances.

When the meditation sitting that is the central part of the initiation began and I closed my eyes, two things happened simultaneously: my Simran (that is, the mental repetition of the mantra which is given to each disciple at initiation) became almost unbearably strong; it was as though my bones and intestines were shouting the Names. I did not feel that I was doing anything; I felt like a trumpet that is being blown through. At the same time I became aware that Baba Sawan Singh, my Master's Master, was standing within in a blaze of brilliant light looking at me with infinite tenderness and compassion. After a few minutes (I have no idea how long, but it was not a very brief period), He turned into my Master, Kirpal Singh. The light was the same, the expression on the face was the same, only the facial features were different. After some time, He changed into Sant Ajaib Singh, Who continued to look at me out of the same light and with the same tenderness. After a while, Baba Sawan Singh returned, and the cycle repeated itself—again and again and again and again, one form followed by another, while my Simran was continuing as strong as before—so strong I felt as though I were a bellows and the Names were being pumped out of me. This continued throughout the sitting, but it didn't stop there—for three glorious days and nights, those three beautiful Radiant Forms were with me whenever I closed my eyes, while my Simran continued to be shouted by the soul of my soul.

From that time I have understood with every ounce of my being that all true Masters are one, that the Master in Ajaib is the same Master that was in Kirpal, and that the road to Rajasthan led directly to my Master's feet.

3. His Mission and Technique

All Masters share the same mission, which has several elements:

1) To take souls which are ready to return to their Source back home;

2) To provide a constant living demonstration that God exists and that He loves us;

3) To show us that that God is our own essence as well as the essence of the universe;

4) To provide us with an alternative way of relating to

each other based on the recognition that "God resides in every heart."

How the Masters accomplish this mission varies from one to another; while they are in essence one, as we have just seen, their personalities and life-roles vary. They have been kings and queens (King Janak, Raja Pipa, Princess Mira-bai), wealthy aristocrats (Swami Ji Maharaj, Dharam Das, Bulleh Shah), multi-lingual scholars with the ability to ad-dress princes, prelates and intellectuals on their own terms (Maulana Rumi, Guru Arjan, Guru Gobind Singh, Baba Sawan Singh, Sant Kirpal Singh). When this has been the case, the outer form of the Master's mission has varied ac-cordingly. But the overwhelming majority of the Masters known to history have been simple uneducated people, sometimes from the lowest strata of society, who earned their living by the labor of their hands and who addressed humanity in simple words made powerful by the magnifi-cence of their soul's achievement. Such was Kabir the weaver, Dhanna the peasant, Shams-i-Tabrez, Shah Inay-at, Sain the barber, Namdev the calico printer, Guru Nanak (a farmer), Ravidas (a cobbler), and Baba Jaimal Singh, who worked thirty-four years as a common soldier. And such also is the living Master Ajaib Singh, the villager from Rajasthan who speaks and writes Punjabi only (he reads and understands Hindi as well), who has worked as a soldier and farmer all his life, whose academic education is minimal, but who speaks with an authority that rever-berates around the world because he has seen God.

One of the striking things about the histories of the Masters is the paradox that those Masters who were wealthy, well-educated and/or of high social status, almost always sat at the feet of Masters who were just the opposite. Thus Maulana Rumi, the proud scholar, was the disciple of

Shams-i-Tabrez, a despised mendicant; Dharam Das, one of the wealthiest Hindus in India, sat at the feet of Kabir, a low-caste Muslim weaver; Bulleh Shah, the high-caste Muslim priest, was initiated by Shah Inayat, an illiterate low-caste peasant. Both Raja Pipa, the King of Gagaraungarh, and Mirabai, the Queen of Chittor, humbled themselves before Ravidas who lived in a hut and who, because he was a cobbler and handled skins of dead animals, was considered unclean by Hindu society. And Baba Sawan Singh, college graduate, military engineer, cavalry officer, sat at the feet of Baba Jaimal Singh, retired infantryman who, like the living Master Ajaib Singh, could speak and write only Punjabi and whose academic education was almost nothing.

The point is that a Master makes use of whatever outer circumstances may be his, but nothing limits his ability to speak directly to the soul of a seeker. When a person is hungering to meet God and really wants it more than anything else, then just seeing a Master is enough to revolutionize his life. I have already told my own feelings when I first encountered Kirpal Singh—how I was overwhelmed with a sense of my own triviality, and how, as I observed Him, I understood this was what human beings were meant to be. This instant reorientation of the seeker by the Master, which I have seen over and over again with both Kirpal and Ajaib, is one of the most impressive aspects of His technique, and is analyzed by Kirpal Singh as follows:

"A system in which the teacher is so central to every aspect of the student's outer and inner discipline and progress and without whose instruction and guidance nothing could be done, must lay great emphasis on the principle of Grace, and mystic literature is not wanting in stressing and underlining this aspect. But if from one angle it is the Master who bestows everything upon the disciple, it must not be forgotten that in doing this he is only repaying a debt he owes to his own Guru, for the gift he bestows is the gift he himself received when he was at the stage of a disciple, and so he usually never claims anything for himself but attributes his power to the grace of his own teacher. Besides, from another angle, everything is in the disciple himself and the Master does not add anything from outside. It is only when the gardener waters and tends the seed that it bursts into life, yet the secret of life is in the seed itself and the gardener can do no more than provide the conditions for its fructification. Such indeed is the function of the Guru.

"An ancient Indian parable vividly brings out this aspect of the Master-disciple relationship. It relates that once a shepherd trapped a lion's cub and reared him with the rest of his flock. The cub, judging himself by those he saw around him, lived and moved like the sheep and lambs, content with the grass they nibbled and with the weak bleats they emitted. And so time sped on until, one day, another lion saw the growing cub grazing with the rest of the flock. He guessed what had happened and pitying the cub's plight, he went up to him, drew him to the side of a quiet stream, made him behold his reflection and the lion's own and, turning back, let forth a mighty roar. The cub, now understanding his true nature, did likewise and his erstwhile companions fled before him. He was at last free to enjoy his rightful place and thenceforward roamed about as a king of the forest.

"The Master is indeed such a lion. He comes to stir up the soul from its slumber and, presenting it with a mirror, makes it behold its own innate glory of which, without his touch, it would continue unaware. However were it not itself of the essence of life, nothing could raise it to spiritual consciousness. The Guru is but a lighted candle that lights the unlit ones. The fuel is there, the wick is there, he only gives the gift of flame without any loss to himself. Like touches like, the spark passes between and that which lay dark is illumined and that which was dead springs into life. As with the lighted candle, whose privilege lies not in its being an individual candle but in its being the seat of the unindividual flame that is neither of this candle nor of that but of the very essence of all fire, so too with the true Master. He is a Master not by virtue of his being an individual master like anyone else, but he is a Master carrying in him the Universal Light of God. Again, just as only a candle that is still burning can light other candles—not one that is already burnt out—so only a living Master can give the quickening touch that is needed, not one who has already departed from this world. Those who are gone are great indeed and worthy of all respect, but they were preeminently for their own time, and the task they accomplished for those around them must, for us, be performed by one who lives and moves in our midst. Their memory is a sacred treasure, a perennial source of inspiration, but the one thing their remembrance teaches is to seek for ourselves in the world of the living that which they themselves were. Only the kiss of a living Prince (Master) could bring the slumbering Princess (Soul) back to life and only the touch of a breathing Beauty could restore the Beast to his native pristine Glory.''[3]

But if showing the seeker what he himself can be is one of the methods the Master uses, it is not the only one. He instructs also, sometimes by hints (especially if the disciple

3. Kirpal Singh, *The Crown of Life*, pp. 174-176

has not asked for advice), but more often by strict blunt instruction that is exactly what the disciple needs to hear—or experience, since it is not always verbal. The following experience occurred in May 1976 at Sant Ji's ashram in Rajasthan, toward the end of the stay. I am quoting directly from a talk given on our return:

"It so happened that I meditated in his presence on two occasions; once at the initiation and once afterwards. And he noticed that I was leaning against the wall, and many other flaws, no doubt.[4] So at some point he said to me, 'After Satsang tonight you follow me.' Pappu (our translator) explained that this was very important and just for me.

"I was really apprehensive. I had no idea what was going to happen. At the appointed time I followed Sant Ji up onto the roof, and I saw his bed—a rope bed—and next to it there was a cushion, on the floor; and he told me to sit on the cushion. I sat; there was no wall anywhere, no way I could lean against anything. And he arranged me with my back just right, my head just right; he said, '*Bheto*,' which means 'sit'; he sent Pappu away, and he sat on his bed and he watched me sit. I sat an hour in that position.

"Within five minutes the pain began in my lower back. It grew and grew and grew until it became all consuming. I couldn't move; he was sitting right there watching me; how could I move? It was not possible. But I wasn't meditating: I was sitting there thinking about my lower back. Then after some time (I had no idea of the time; it seemed like I was

4. The first meditation was the one where the gates opened for me, as I described above. The second was after it was over. The fact that I still had a lot to learn about meditation technique only underscores the principle of Grace—that that transcendent experience had had nothing to do with any qualities of mine, but was simply a gift.

there for twenty-four hours) one of my legs began to hurt; and that very quickly made my lower back seem like nothing at all. The pain in my leg became excruciating. I was sitting there hurting in my back, hurting in my leg, totally divorced from anything that I had ever thought about in connection with meditation. Every ounce of my being was concentrated on not moving.

"Finally Sant Ji called Pappu and told me to leave off. He looked at me with infinite compassion, and asked me about pain—where it hurt. I told him. He didn't ask about my meditation; He knew exactly where I was that night on that score. I was rubbing my leg like anything, and he asked me if I would like a massage. He was so gentle and compassionate. I said no, it would be all right. 'All right,' he said, 'tomorrow night you will come up again.' And he sent me off.

"The second night it had been raining, and we sat inside his room. I was getting a cold again by this time; the pneumonia that I had had just before I went began to come back again at the very end of the trip. So the second night it was the same, except it was worse. And I moved some; I couldn't help it. I didn't squirm or shuffle but I stretched out my back and then I lowered it down and I moved around and tried to crack my neck. (When we meditate, you know, we are not aware of how many times we move. When we sit in our own lazy way leaning against something, we might even be doing well; but if something occurs to us, we don't even think twice—we simply move our leg a little bit, or whatever. I think there are thousands of movements that most of us make without even being aware of it. This is my experience; based on all of a sudden being made aware of it, you see.)

"So the second night was worse than the first; it was

awful. I was ashamed because I had moved, and the pain was worse; especially the back pain. Every muscle of my lower back was rebelling and shrieking against having to hold me up. And when Sant Ji took me out this time, I questioned him: 'Sant Ji, I am not saying this is something I ought not to be doing; I sense that this is a very important thing that I have to learn. But I have had very good and fruitful meditations using a back support. Is it absolutely necessary to sit like this?'

"He said, 'It's not necessary at all. You don't have to do it. You don't have to come up here either; you can sit down on your bed at this hour, if you like. You can meditate any way you like.' But he added very humbly, 'I have found that this way has been helpful to me, and I would also like to see you do it. If you can get proficient at this you will find, first, that you will never get sleepy. You will be able to meditate for hours without sleeping. And, second, your progress will be greatly accelerated. This is my view.'

"He was very humble, and there was no question of ordering or forcing, although I understood very clearly from within that I had to do this: that this was something that I should have learned years ago.

"I asked him, 'How long will it take? It's like I'm not meditating. I'm sitting here but I'm thinking only about not moving and having pain. How long will it take before I'm meditating again?' He said, 'Ten to fifteen days should do it, if you sit an hour and a half daily in this position when you get home at least; and a half an hour in bhajan.' I said, 'All right.' I thought I'd never do it. And I went down.

"On the third night I was following Sant Ji up the stairs when I realized that I didn't have any kleenex with me. I had a bad cold by then and I needed to blow my nose constantly. And while I was prepared not to blow it during the meditation, I thought that I should at least get a good blow before I started. But I had somehow neglected to put any in my pocket. I was already following him up the stairs, and I couldn't turn around and run back for the kleenex—it seemed so much what he was weaning me away from. So I thought, 'All right, Master, I'll do it. Whatever I have to do, I'll do.'

"Now I'm telling this story in the full realization that I should have learned all this years and years ago. In my trips to India Master used to look at me sometimes when I'd sit against the wall. And I knew that he would prefer me not to. And also many times I did sit without a back support, but I sat hunched over, moving a lot. I just chose to think it didn't matter.

"The third night was on the roof again. We sat there. Now when Sant Ji would call me up he was in his underwear. He had some kind of little loin-cloth and a T-shirt, and his turban off. It was a very different visual impression from when he was wearing his clothes and his turban.

"I had to blow my nose. Before I even started, I had to blow it. *And I'm telling you the third night it began to work*. From beginning to end, I did not have any pain. That was the first thing. The effort to keep still was enormous; with all my being I had to work on that. But I was able to do it. I didn't move once the third night. And I actually meditated, this is the point. The withdrawal process began and with it came experience which I would not have believed possible considering the circumstances, where my attention was and how I was sitting. But it was like just enough had been accomplished so that everything started to happen and it was beautiful.

"When Sant Ji took me out, there was a stream of mucous—one long stream—down to my lap. And I had not been aware of it; it had happened by itself. I just didn't know it was there until I came out of meditation. I had a note in my pocket that someone had given me and I blew my nose on that note because I had to do something. I was terribly excited and I turned around and Sant Ji asked me what was going on. And I told him that tonight there was no pain, that meditation had been possible, the withdrawal process had begun. I told him what had happened inside and what I had seen. And he listened. He said, 'Good.' And I said, 'I hope that when I go home I will have discipline enough so I can do this without your sitting there, right there, watching me.' Because I understood it was because of his interest, the fact that he was watching me, that enabled me to do it. He said, 'Never think for one minute that I am not watching you.' Which I should have known anyway, you know.

"And I started to get up. And I looked at this figure sitting there, in his underwear and his T-shirt without his turban, sitting on the bed, who had just taken me through some kind of rebirth experience, during which something that had been crystalized had been broken. (Some teachings have this theory that wrong crystalization can take place and then it has to be broken forcibly in order for further progress to happen. I felt like that had happened.) I couldn't see him well in the darkness, his face was hidden. I couldn't even see his eyes. I could only see his white beard in the moonlight. But his greatness and power overwhelmed me and spontaneously from my heart I leaned forward; I went down and bumped my head on the floor and reached out to touch his feet—which was the first time I tried to do that. He was up off that bed in a second. He grabbed me around the waist and pulled me up to a sitting position. He was laughing. He said, 'Don't do that. Never do that.' And he picked me up so that I was standing and he put his arm around me and led me to the stairs. And he said, 'Have a good rest tonight.' And he sent me off. And that was the last night we were there.

"I knew when I went in February Master dragged me there because I had to learn something for my growth. And when I met him and talked to him, I heard my Master talking to me and I knew I had to listen. He was telling me at that time what I needed to learn about the whole business relating to the succession and to the fighting and the quarreling among satsangis. And I listened; I knew my Master was talking to me.

"And this time he dragged me over there because I had to learn something else. And I don't mean just sitting still, although that's a part of it. *But the Path is a real thing*. We walk it like dilettantes. But the Saints, all of the Saints, and their real devotees—for them it's a ruling passion. It's the reality. Other things come into play only in order to make the reality possible. In daily life we forget this. Even if we've supposedly devoted our life to Master, to His cause, to His service, even then. And this is what I needed to understand—the ruling passion that enables you to sit even if your leg goes into the fire, even if ants are biting you: because you care more about finding God than you care about your leg. That kind of thing is what takes a person to Sach Khand in this very lifetime. And as Master said, 'Those who have done it can help someone do it. And the world is not without them but they are rare always.'

"So I was outwardly dragged there this time for some reason or other connected with trips and organizations and his coming and this and that. But inwardly, because I needed to learn something. And I needed to learn it badly. And, with the Grace of God, I've learned it . . . I hope. That's all I can say."

CHAPTER FOUR

Holy Initiation

When a Master gives initiation He is opening the first door
into the initiate's Self. There are many doors, but the first
one is pivotal: if that is not opened, then how can we reach
the others?

If, as the Masters say, our soul is of the same essence as
God, then it would follow that when the door opens into
our Self that we would catch a glimpse of God. And that is
exactly what happens. According to the Masters, when the
Absolute God (*Anami* or *Radhasoami*) came into expression at the stage of Sach Khand, It projected Itself as Light
and Sound; and by means of this Light and Sound (con-
ceived of as twin manifestations of one basic creative force,
known most commonly as *Naam* or *Shabda*—"Name" or
"Word" or "Sound Current") the entire created universe
was brought into being. But it is incorrect to understand the
creation as being separate from the Creator: the *Naam* or
"Word" is not only the means used to fashion the universe,
it is also that from which it is fashioned. It is the presence of
this *Naam*—that is, the projection or expression of God—
at the core of every creature that gives it life, and it is its
withdrawal from any creature that causes death. That is
why it is said that "God resides in every heart"; not just as a
poetic fancy, but as a plain statement of fact—and not just
for human beings, but for all created life.

Since the facet of God that constitutes the core or essence
of each living creature is the projected Light and Sound that

characterize the creative force called *Naam*, it follows that if a person knew how and where to look, he or she would literally be able to see and hear the outer manifestation of the Creator within his or her own Self. And this is exactly what Master does for us at the time of initiation: He shows us how and where to look and listen, so that we may see and hear for ourselves the outermost direct manifestation of the creative force that is the projection or expression of the Absolute.

Initiation can also be understood as a double commitment on the part of both the disciple and the Master. The disciple makes a solemn promise to the universe that he is through fooling around, that he understands his true purpose, and that he will do nothing to undermine it; and the universe does him the honor of taking him seriously. Once that promise is made, the disciple cannot unmake it; it is not possible to "leave the Path" in any meaningful sense. Since the Path encompasses the scope and essence of life, where could one go? If the effort is made to leave it, as sometimes happens (for instance, in my own life, as explained above) it is at a terrible price. This is why the Path is compared to a razor's edge; this is why Kirpal Singh has written:

"No Master has ever been interested in attracting large numbers to himself and quantity has never been my aim. It is quality that counts and I would rather have a handful of disciples—nay, even one—who can sacrifice his ego on the spiritual altar and learn to live by love, than millions who understand not the value and meaning of these virtues. I have suggested this before and I emphasize it again, that a seeker should be studied more carefully and his/her background learned more before being recommended for initiation. If after understanding the basic principles of the science, he is willing to undertake this complete remolding

of himself that its practice requires, then and then alone can
he become a fit recipient of initiation."[1]

The Master also makes a commitment to the disciple: that
he will take him to the Court of God by the quickest possible means, and be fully responsible for him on the journey.
The Master lives up to His commitment regardless of
whether the disciple lives up to his; that is precisely why it is
important that the disciple *does* live up to his. If he does
not, he may find himself being dragged along the Path by
his neck. Once we invite the Master into our lives, He is
there; we can't un-invite Him. Once we are "born again," in
Jesus's terminology, we are born; how can we be unborn?

The initiation process itself is performed by the living
Master in person or, in distant countries, by an authorized
representative. The power is exactly the same in both cases,
and a person initiated by an authorized representative acting under the Master's orders is just as initiated as a person
who receives the instructions at the Master's physical feet.
The practice of using representatives in far away places is a
relatively recent phenomenon, dating from 1911, when
Baba Sawan Singh authorized Kehr Singh Sasmus to give
the instructions to Dr. and Mrs. H. M. Brock of Port
Angeles, Washington—as far as I know, the first Western
initiates into Sant Mat ever. Since then a large percentage of
the western initiates have received Naam from the representatives.

The initiation itself is often given in the early hours of the
morning and takes about four hours from start to finish.
Careful instruction into the three meditation practices of
Surat Shabd Yoga (*Simran, Dhyan, Bhajan*) as well as some
explanation of the theory of Sant Mat is given; the mantra
of the Five Holy Names is conveyed and memorized; and

1. Kirpal Singh, *The Way of the Saints*, p.313

two separate meditation sittings are held, during which a demonstration in practice of what has previously been explained in theory is given. During these sittings, under the watchful eye of the Master or his representative, the new initiate puts into practice for the first time the instructions he has just received, and experiences for himself both the withdrawal of the spirit from the body and the seeing and hearing of the inner Light and Sound—may be little or more, depending on the background and receptivity of the initiate. After the sittings, he has an opportunity to analyze his first meditation practice and discuss it with the Master of His representative, clear up anything he does not understand, and receive additional instruction for the future based on his experience for the first time. If for any reason there is an obstruction (usually nervous tension) which prevents him from carrying out the instructions accurately, he is given an opportunity to sit again, after the instructions are over, with special attention paid to his own particular difficulty. He can ask any question he wishes, and does not in fact leave until all questions are answered. Needless to say, this process (which is called *Naam-Daan* or the "giving of Naam" in Hindi) is free and open to anyone who really wants it—enough to fulfill the preliminary requirements.

The theory which is explained to the new initiate at this time is the basic cosmology of the Masters—a view of the universe astoundingly different than any known to orthodox western thought, although it was the world view of the Pythagoreans, Neo-Platonists, Gnostics, Sufis and Kabbalists. The Masters say that there are "planes" or levels of being in addition to the physical—eight altogether, in fact, although the number may vary depending on how classification is being made. These planes represent different manifestations of the Naam, or Creative Power, as it descended from the Absolute stage. The nearest to the physical, what is often called the "astral plane," is well-known to yogis and occultists and has been the subject of much speculation and interest. Because it has certain points in common with the physical plane, and is not as difficult to reach as the ones above it, it has been often discussed. The fact is, however, that to actually "reach" the astral plane, so that one is existing and functioning from that level of awareness, is no small thing, and very few of those who talk freely about it have actually reached there. In addition, the astral plane is only the beginning; existing and functioning on the astral level is not *Nirvana* or *Moksha* (liberation from birth or death), is not above the Law of Karma, and in fact, insofar as it contributes to the feeling of spiritual success that is another form of egoism, can even work *against* the ultimate attaining of Nirvana or liberation. The Masters have their own ways of dealing with these problems and those disciples who remain humbly and trustingly in their care are protected from this difficulty. This is one reason why it is absolutely essential for a serious meditator or spiritual practitioner to have a Master: strenuous intensive work on one's own can do a lot, but it cannot conquer the ego. It only strengthens it. As long as we can think, "I have done it, I am doing it, I can do it," then the I-hood remains and grows stronger, ultimately limiting our achievement and preventing further progress.

The organ that allows us to experience the astral plane is the "astral body," which in fact is our "ghost." The astral body is sometimes visible to the physical eye, and it looks something like our physical body; when we withdraw finally and completely from the physical body, it is the astral body that emerges as our outer covering, and it is suited for life on the astral level just as our physical body is suited for

life on the physical level. Once in a while someone manages
to withdraw from the physical body and function in the
astral body *on the physical plane*. This is called "astral projection," and it unquestionably happens; but it is a freakish
occurrence, not beneficial to anyone, and does not lead
anywhere. Sometimes when a person dies, if there is a
strong attachment to some particular place or person on the
physical plane, the conscious entity of the deceased,
wrapped in its astral body, may continue for a while in the
vicinity of that place or person; this is what has given rise to
the stories of "ghosts." Again there is no question that it
happens; but such occurrences are also freakish, and such
ghosts are unfortunate creatures, deserving compassion
and pity rather than fear or hatred.

Above the astral plane (or more correctly, surrounding,
enveloping and interpenetrating the astral plane) is the
"causal plane," the fountainhead of phenomena as we
understand it. And, just as we have an astral body that
enables us to function in the astral plane, so do we have a
causal body that enables us to function in the causal plane.
Neither this plane nor this body is describable in terms that
are meaningful to us (apart from its essential light and
sound, which are described at initiation) but the Masters say
that this causal body is also called the "seed body" because
the seeds of much that we look upon as irrevocably part of
ourselves are in fact part of it. Our mind, including the sub-
conscious reservoir of our past impressions; the three *gunas*
or innate tendencies (*satva* or peace; *rajas* or activity; *tamas*
or inertia); our desires and fears, which bind us to the Karmic wheel and the cycle of births and deaths—all have their
seeds in this body and at this stage. We think of all these
things as part of our "Selves"; but when we reach this point
in our inner journey we see clearly that they are not. We see

for ourselves that our "Selves" and our "minds" are two distinct entities and that the mind, which has usurped our identity, in reality derives its energy from the soul and is not of our essence at all. This discovery marks the beginning of true "Self-knowledge" or "Self-realization"; before this point, we cannot know what our "Self" is.

The causal plane is also the seat of that particular aspect of God whom the Masters call Kal or the Negative Power. The mind in fact is seen as a spark or drop of the flame or ocean of the Negative Power in the same way as the soul is a spark or drop of the Supreme Father or Positive Power. This Negative Power is known to many traditions, including the Judean-Christian-Islamic, as some sort of Devil figure, or embodiment of absolute evil; but there is only a greater or lesser absence or covering up of good. Far from being a separate and equal (or almost equal) counterpart of the good God, Kal is in fact a created being like the rest of us who is carrying out a necessary part of the whole. Far from being absolutely evil, he is absolutely fair and just; the whole of the "three worlds" (physical, astral and causal planes), under his control, are governed strictly according to the Law of Karma—"as you sow, so shall you reap." There is no possiblity of appealing to Kal's mercy, because he has none. It is not difficult to understand how, to sinners who deserved heavy penalties for their sins and who appealed in vain for forgiveness, Kal appeared as evil.

The Negative Power also figures as a tempter, working through the mind seeking to prevent the spiritual aspirant from rising above his realm. Why? Because strictly speaking, no one *deserves* to rise higher; it is only the mercy and grace of the Positive Power, working through the living Master, which makes it possible. That is why it is said that Kal is only doing his duty when he tries to prevent us from going within; but of course he appears evil to those who are being tempted by him.

The stage above the causal plane, called *Daswan Dwar* or the "tenth door" by the Masters, and sometimes referred to as the "super-causal plane," is the first region that is beyond the reach of the Negative Power or the mind. Hence it is a very important point in the inner journey, and those who reach this far are called *sadhu*. This is the real meaning of this term; its application to the thousands of wandering monks in India is an error. A real Sadhu is a very high soul indeed; he or she can even act as a guru if necessary and if ordered to do so.

Two planes above Daswan Dwar is the fifth plane, referred to by the Masters as *Sach Khand* or *Sat Lok*. This is the stage at which God appears in His fullness as *Sat Purush* or the Positive Power; this is the highest form of God that can be called "personal." There are three stages above this, but the God Who exists in these stages cannot be related to or described in any way; it cannot even be meaningfully said that He exists.

It is the Sat Purush Who is called the Supreme Father and Who is best described as an Ocean of Love. It is the Sat Purush Who comes into the world in the human form of the true Masters. Further, it is the Sat Purush Who has created the whole manifest universe out of His essence (although that represents only a tiny part of It) and Who is thus the very soul of our soul. And when the soul reaches the stage of Sach Khand and sees the Positive Power in His full glory, it realizes that God, the Master, and itself are all one and the same.

This fifth plane is the goal that the Master lays before the disciple, and it is as far as He takes him. One who reaches here is a Saint indeed; the Sanskrit/Hindi/Punjabi word

Sant, which is the root of our English word "saint," means just that: one who has reached Sach Khand, the fifth plane. The soul can go higher; it can trace the thread of manifestation all the way back to the eighth or final stage of the Absolute, but the Master does not take one; the Master as such has ceased to exist at the fifth plane, so God Himself takes one into the core of His essence. One who journeys this far is called *Param Sant*—supreme saint, saint of saints—but from the point of view of the disciple there is no way to differentiate between a *Sant* and a *Param Sant*, nor is there any need to bother. Either is capable of taking the disciple to Sach Khand.

Do these planes really exist? Some of the mystics who have described their inner experiences—Jaluluddin Rumi, Kabir, Nanak, Tulsidas, Ramakrishna—are well known, but scholars from Arthur Waley to Morton Smith have persisted in referring to these experiences as "hallucinations." Are they right? When I was searching for truth and first initiated I was bothered by this question. I was once explaining the inner planes to a friend of mine and he became agitated and said, "You know, Russell, there are plenty of people in mental hospitals who believe just this." I coughed politely and changed the subject. But it bothered me. I thought it through and came up with a many-sided answer: First of all, there is a long tradition of belief in these planes, in the importance of the Naam or Word, and in the various manifestations of God found therein, especially the Positive and Negative Powers, and in the Law of Karma and the cycle of births and deaths. *Sant Mat* is the name that is applied to this teaching's manifestation in modern India (from the thirteenth century on) but the teaching itself is older than old. The Christian Gnostics certainly taught it, as did the Jewish Kabbalists; the same basic ideas are found

among the Muslim Sufis, Taoists and the Mahayana Bud-
dhists. The testimony is consistent and long-lived, not confined to any one religion or even culture; and the Masters of
all these traditions have sometimes been very specific, for
while disciples are usually forbidden to speak of what they
have experienced within, the Masters are not.

Secondly, what manner of person is it who is bearing
testimony to these things? Well, some of them are obscure,
especially the ancient ones; some of them, like the Gnostics
and other Christian "heretics," have had an extremely bad
press, since they were on what according to history was the
losing side; but many of them are well-known indeed.
Jalaluddin Rumi, the man universally considered to be the
greatest Sufi of them all, is also by common consent the
greatest poet in the Persian language. He is the author of an
epic of cosmic proportions, the *Masnavi*, perhaps the most
remarkable poem in any literature, and the *Divan of
Shams-i-Tabrez*, a book of exquisite lyrics. During his
lifetime he was an advisor to princes as well as ordinary people, and had Jewish and Christian disciples as well as
Muslims (no small feat in the Middle Ages) and was considered a great Islamic intellectual theologian as well as a
great mystic. Does a life like this sound like it was founded
on hallucinations?

Kabir is another case in point. A Muslim weaver (*julaha*),
one of the lowest castes in India, he came to rival the
Brahmins in influence and prestige. He had thousands of
Hindu disciples and is honored today as the founder of a
sect (the *Kabir-panth*) to which a million northern Hindus
belong, yet he never stopped being a Muslim! Hundreds of
stories are extant about him and they are remarkably consistent: they bear collective testimony to a strong, powerful,
yet humble person, compassionate, blunt, clear of intellect;

a personality so vivid that when Christian missionaries tried to convert Kabir-panthis, they found that they were unable to comprehend in what way Christ was superior to, or different from, Kabir. And Kabir is considered generally to be the greatest Hindi lyric poet; thousands of his songs have been preserved and are still sung today all over northern India. Is it not more difficult to believe that such a life could be solidly based on a foundation of hallucination than it is to believe that Kabir had solved the mystery of life?

Kirpal Singh has commented on this matter as follows:

"Many modern scholars, more so those with Western modes of thought, have, when first confronted by yoga, tended to dismiss it as no more than an elaborate means of self-hypnotism. Such an attitude is quite unscientific even though it often parades under the garb of science. It is generally the result of prejudice born of ignorance or a superficial knowledge of the subject. It is natural for us to attempt to relegate to the realm of superstition, phenomena with which we are unfamiliar and which defy our habitual ways of thought about life, for to study them, to understand them, to test and accept them, would require effort and perseverance of which most of us are incapable. It is not unlikely that some so-called yogins may justify the label of 'self-hypnotists.' But those few who genuinely merit the name of yogins are too humble to court publicity and have nothing about them to suggest the neurotic escapist. They invariably display a remarkably sensitive awareness to life in all its complexity and variety, and this awareness coupled with their humility makes all talk of self-delusion quite inapt, irrelevant and even ridiculous. For, to seek the Unchanging behind the changing, the Real behind the phenomenal, is certainly not to 'hypnotize' oneself. If anything it displays a spirit of enquiry that is exceptional in its honesty and integrity, that is content with nothing less than the absolute truth, and the kind of renunciation it demands is most difficult to practice. Hence it is, that as time passes, as knowledge is gradually undermining ignorance, the former philistinism is steadily wearing away. The new developments of the physical sciences have had no small share in furthering this process, for by revealing that everything in this physical universe is relative and that matter is not matter per se but ultimately a form of energy, it has confirmed, at the lower level of the yogic concept at least, the conception of the world inherent in the yogic system, giving it a scientific validity which was earlier doubted."[2]

I have already described my initial subjective reactions to both Kirpal Singh and Ajaib Singh, and told something of my continuing relationship to them. At one point, this question popped into my mind when I was sitting with Kirpal, and I just looked at the Master and laughed. I thought, "I'm with Him. If He got to be like this by self-hypnosis and hallucinations, then bring them on. Whatever He is, I want to be." As Jesus said, "Ye shall know them by their fruits. Do men gather grapes of thorns, or figs of thistles? . . . A good tree cannot bring forth evil fruit, neither can a corrupt tree bringeth forth good fruit . . . Wherefore by their fruits ye shall know them."[3]

The final facet of this answer is eloquently stated by the great French writer and thinker, Romain Rolland:

2. Kirpal Singh, *The Crown of Life,* pp. 82-83; see also *The Tao of Physics* by Fritjof Capra.

3. Matthew 7: 16, 18, 20

". . . the careful study of mysticism establishes clearly that consciousness exists undimmed in this gigantic ascent backwards up the ladder of the past [i.e., the return to the Source], compared to which Wells's *Time Machine* is mere child's play; and M. F. Morel [a psychologist] comes back to it on several occassions:

" 'In the most complete introversion . . . there is no loss of consciousness, but a displacement of attention . . . Ecstatic experiences remain deeply engraven upon those who experience them, and this would not be the case if they were simply empty or devoid of meaning. . . . When the exterior world has disappeared, the circle of consciousness contracts and seems to withdraw entirely into some unknown and ignored cortical centre. Consciousness seems to gather itself together to confine itself within some unknown psychic pineal gland and to withdraw into a kind of center wherein all organic functions and all psychic forces meet, and there it enjoys Unity . . . nothing else.' (Morel, Essay on Mystic Intraversion, p. 112)

" 'Nothing else?'—What more do you want? There, according to your own admission, you have an instrument for penetrating to the depths of functional consciousness, of subliminal life—and yet you do not use it in order to complete your knowledge of the whole activity of the mind. You, doctors of the Unconscious, instead of making yourselves citizens of this boundless empire and possessing yourselves of it, do you ever enter it except as foreigners, imbued with the preconceived idea of the superiority of your own country and incapable of ridding yourselves of the need, which itself deforms your vision, of reducing whatever you catch a glimpse of in this unknown world to the measure of the one already familiar to you?

"Think of the extraordinary interest of these striking descriptions—a succession of Indian, Alexandrine and Christian mystics of all sects without mutual knowledge of each other have all with the same lucidity gone through the same experiences. . . . Is it a slight thing by means of direct inner perception to be able to realize the great cosmic laws and the forces that govern the universe controlled by our senses?

"If a scientist maintains that such a knowledge of psychic profundities teaches us nothing about exterior realities, he is really, though perhaps unwittingly, obeying a prejudice of proud incomprehension as one-eyed as that of religious spiritualists who set up an insurmountable barrier between spirit and matter. . . . There are not two realities. That which exists in one exists in the other. The laws of the inner psychic substance are of necessity those of outside reality. And if you succeed in reading one properly, the chances are that you will find the confirmation and if not, the presentiment of what you have read or will read in the other . . .

"But if this is true, the judicious use of deep introversion opens to the scientist unexplored resources: for it constitutes a new method of experiment, having the advantage that the observer identifies himself with the object observed —the Plotinian identity of the seer and the thing seen."[4]

At the beginning of the book, I mentioned that I had experienced the "conversion" that evangelicals refer to as being "born again," but that I did not feel that this was what Jesus meant by that phrase. My own experiences led me to the conclusion years ago that both the references to being "born again" (found only in the third chapter of the Gospel

4. Romain Rolland, *The Life of Vivekananda and the Universal Gospel*, pp. 341-344

of John) and to "baptism," in particular, Jesus's baptism, refer to an initiation which Jesus had himself received from John the Baptist and which he then, after a period of meditation in the wilderness, passed on to others. The word "baptise" comes from a Greek word meaning "immerse"; when John speaks of one who will "baptise you with the Holy Spirit," he is saying literally, "immerse you in the Holy Spirit." It seemed clear to me that the water baptism described in the Bible was only an outer form symbolic of the inner experience. I could not prove this, of course; but as I read the Gospels over and over, it became very clear that if we accepted the hypothesis that Jesus was initiating his disciples into the inner mysteries, all the pieces in the Gospels that now seem so contradictory and inconsistent would fit together. For years I studied this question, finding scraps of evidence which pointed in this direction; then the discovery by Professor Morton Smith of an authentic letter of the Church Father, Clement of Alexandria, quoting extensively from a secret Gospel of Mark in which Jesus is unmistakably giving initiation, proved it beyond a shadow of doubt. Clement's letter shows exactly how the secret Gospel was fitted in and around our present-day Gospel of Mark (and incidentally, explains why Mark is so abrupt and choppy, despite its vivid and intimate style, since what we have is an abridgment) and connects Jesus with the Gnostics. [5]

The Gnostics—"those who knew"—were early Christians who believed in the necessity of a living Master, the cycle of births and deaths or reincarnation, the Positive and

5. See Morton Smith, *The Secret Gospel*, pp. 14-17. Scholars may prefer to consult *Clement of Alexandria and the Secret Gospel of Mark*, by the same author, which is much more detailed and contains the original Greek text. While I consider Prof. Smith's work of the utmost importance, I disagree most emphatically with many of his conclusions.

Negative Powers, and who taught a meditation technique into which one was initiated and through which one was enabled to rise above body consciousness and enter the inner planes. The similarity of these ideas with those of Sant Mat is obvious. The Gnostic Masters traced their spiritual descent directly to Jesus, sometimes through Simon Magus. Gnosticism was anathema to most of the Church Fathers, who considered it "elitist"—a misunderstanding—and decadent—which may in some cases have been true. When the orthodox official Church assumed secular power under Constantine the Great, they embarked on a program of stamping out the Gnostics and blackening their names, including re-writing the Book of Acts to, among other things, portray Simon Magus as a villain. The Church succeeded very well, and to this day "Gnostic" is a dirty word among orthodox Christians.[6]

One final point on the initiation: Often in Sant Mat literature reference is made to the *Panch Shabd* or the *Panch Naam*—i.e., the Five Sounds or the Five Names. As the creative Current which the Masters call *Naam* (Name) or *Shabd* (Sound) comes down from Sach Khand, it creates and sustains a number of planes or levels of consciousness or inner universes of varying degrees of density. At each level, the creative Current emits a characteristic Sound which is heard by those who have reached that level or are close to it. Since there are five major inner planes, there are five basic Sounds proceeding from the one Current. Since the Current is the manifestation of Divine activity, the Sounds are often referred to as the Five Names—God nam-

6. For an excellent and sympathetic overview of the Gnostics, see G.R.S. Mead, *Fragments of a Faith Forgotten—The Gnostics: A Study of the Origins of Christianity.* Elaine Pagels' recent *The Gnostic Gospels* is also helpful.

ing Himself. The mantra of Five Names that is given at initiation is based on the inner Five Sounds and closely connected with them—as closely as human speech will allow. Therefore those Names are referred to as the "Basic Names of God" as opposed to attributive or descriptive names[7] (although many great mystics have coined such names). At the time of initiation, the mantra of Basic Names is given, the inner Sounds to which those Names refer are described, and some experience of actually hearing one or more of those Sounds is given. That is why it is often referred to as "Initiation into the Five Sounds."

7. See Kirpal Singh, *The Way of the Saints*, pp. 109-111.

CHAPTER FIVE

Spiritual Discipline

Initiation is given, free of charge, to anyone who really
wants it; that is a principle of the Masters that is always
valid. But in order for it to work—in order for the seed that
is sown to thrive and develop and grow—the life of the initiate has to be lived in accordance with the instructions of the
Master. These instructions encompass all areas of life, and
they are no small thing: if they are ignored or forgotten,
even in part, real progress will be impossible and meditation
will be in vain. But it is important to remember that this is
why the instructions are given and the discipline is to be
maintained: because failure affects meditation and prevents
progress. They are not arbitrary pronouncements handed
down from on high, nor do they proceed from someone's
conception of social needs.

The Masters often divide the essentials of spiritual discipline into five categories: 1) Non-violence (*Ahimsa*), 2) Truthfulness (*Satayam*), 3) Chastity (*Brahmcharya*), 4) Universal Love (*Prem*), 5) Selfless Service (*Nishkam Seva*).
They advise the disciple to practice self-introspection—that
is, to remain in a state of *remembrance*, or consciousness
sufficient to enable him to be aware that he is failing in any
of the categories. The practice of *Simran*—repetition of the
mantra of Five Names given at initiation—is the primary
means to this end: if one part of the mind is engaged in
Simran, it acts as a non-participating observer and sees immediately when the rest of the self is ready to fall. Since

199

most of our failures in any category are due to un-
consciousness or forgetfulness—Kirpal Singh has written,
"Saints give a very simple definition of sin as 'forgetting
one's origin' (or God-head)"[1]—the practice of Simran
works to counteract that forgetting or sleep by keeping one
part of us constantly awake. Then, instead of observing us
in the process of failing through the lens of self-justification
which is our habit, we will see it as it really is. Anger will be
seen as anger first, and the cause that justifies it will come
after—a reversal of the usual process. Because we are
remembering who we really are and what we are trying to
achieve, we will care more about becoming angry than
about whatever insult or slight or wrong that has provoked
the anger; we will care more because we will remember that
we will be sitting for meditation that night and a loss of
temper, even a minor one, can shatter us so much that we
will not have a peaceful meditation for days. And so with
each of the five categories: indulgence or slipping into any
of them means a dead stop on the Path, nothing less. That is
why they are so important.

To make the practice of self-introspection easier, the
Masters have adopted different ways at different times. Kirpal Singh introduced a "diary form"—a sheet of paper
with the categories listed down one side and boxes for each
day of the month, arranged so the number of failures in
each category could be conveniently listed.[2] It also included
space for keeping track of the amount of time spent in
meditation each day and, at the end of the month, what the
fruits of meditation are and what the problems or difficulties seem to be. If kept correctly, this diary is a complete

1. Kirpal Singh, *The Wheel of Life,* p. 37

2. Actually very similar to forms used by St. Ignatius Loyola and Ben-
jamin Franklin, among others.

and accurate record of the disciple's state of consciousness over a month's time, and if he feels that his progress is insufficient, the reason can be found there.

If kept correctly. There's the rub. The diary is only as effective as the consciousness that is keeping it. Kirpal Singh has written:

"Unfortunately few, if any, have any idea of what keeping the diary really means. As time passes, their entries become a mere matter of form, and the whole purpose behind keeping the diary is lost. We are asked to maintain the diary in thought, word and deed. How many of us really do so? The majority just react in thought, word and deed to the stimulus of the moment, in other words, instinctively. The truth of the matter is that we must become consciously aware of every thought that passes through the mind; we must weigh our words before we speak and not speak idle words as a mere reaction to the situation that confronts us. If we are able to make some progress in this regard, then we will be far on the way to controlling our self. This in essence is the practice of Raja Yoga. Only when we have advanced far in the practice of living the life demanded of us (as implied in the keeping of the diary) will we become fit enough to reap the fruits of the practices of the Surat Shabd Yoga."[3]

The diary form is for the benefit of the disciple and it is for him to read; nevertheless, for many years Kirpal Singh requested the initiates to send Him their completed diaries at regular intervals of three to four months. One year before

3. From a letter, published by the New York Satsang. For further comments, see Kirpal Singh, *The Way of the Saints*, especially pp. 95-131 (on Simran as remembrance), pp. 370-373, and 379-385.

His final samadhi, He altered those instructions (except in special cases), pointing out that in reality the diaries are for *our* benefit, and implying that the main purpose in having them sent to Him was to give us an impetus to keep them. Ajaib Singh has continued in this way, instructing the initiates to keep the diary but not necessarily to send the completed forms to Him. He has also, like Kirpal Singh, laid great emphasis on the *purpose* of the practice of self-introspection, distinguishing clearly the means from the ends. While on tour in the United States, someone asked Ajaib Singh to comment on keeping the diary. He replied as follows:

"Once Guru Gobind Singh went to a town named Roop Nagar in the Punjab. And there many satsangis came to him. Guru Gobind Singh asked them, 'Have you counted your sins?' Then they replied, 'We are illiterate and we cannot keep any account.' At that time in India, only a few were learned, one out of thousands. But Masters have their own ways of explaining things to the disciples; they have many ways. So Guru Gobind Singh told them, 'When you fail in anything, when you make any mistake, you take one stone and put it aside. At the end of the day you count all the stones: how many stones are there and how many piles you have done.' When they had practiced this for a month, there was a big heap of stones. And when they all met again, they said, 'This is a very great burden. How will we finish off this burden? How will we stop all these bad mistakes? Our Master has to finish off all this.'' So they made up their minds that from then onward they would not do any mistakes and they would not collect any more stones.

"After some time when Guru Gobind Singh again went there to do satsang, he asked the disciples: 'Yes, have you kept the accounts?' They said, 'Yes, we kept account for one month and we collected a lot of stones; but now we have decided that we will not collect any more stones because we will not do any more faults.' They obeyed the commandments of Guru Sahib for only one month and in that one month they perfected themselves.

"The same power sat in the body of Kirpal and He advised us, He taught us, according to the means going on in the world at this time. He told us to keep an account of our sins. You are learned people, so you can keep the diary. But it is a pity that some people who are initiated 25 years back, or 30 years back, are still filling out the diary forms; and the sin which we have done in the last month, we are again repeating that.

"In India, in the villages, if anyone has to decide any lawsuit, five people of the villages get together and they decide. And it is a proverb that when those five people make any decision, the man to whom this decision is applied, he says, 'Yes, well, I am welcoming this decision'; but when the five elders go away, he does not do what was decided.

"Now we are filling in the diary forms but we are not giving up our faults. I tell you that if you keep account for one month, and you see how much meditation you have done and how many sins you have done, if you are really sincere, you will not need to fill out the diary forms again. We understand this as ceremony or custom—to fill the diary forms. But whatever we are writing in the diary, we are not following that. We should weed out the faults with love, with the same love with which we record the mistake. According to the Masters, if everyone had kept the diary, all the souls would not be trapped, would not be deluded in the regions of mind, and Master would have manifested within them.

"When I was initiated by Master, I was initiated in a separate room; and in the other room where the other people were being initiated I saw that they were given diary forms. So I requested, 'Give me the form so that I can also keep the diary.' But Master replied, 'Your life is your diary.'

"So we should mould our lives according to the diary. Master had not given us the diary to just keep filling up as a daily account. If we will keep the accounts sincerely for one month and count all the sins, our soul will tremble at how many sins, how many faults we have done in that month."[4]

With this in mind let us look at the five cardinal virtues one by one and see what the Masters are calling us to.

1. Non-Violence (Ahimsa)

The conscientious practice of all the five virtues has only one aim, and it is the same as the practice of meditation: the ultimate annihilation of the personal ego, or I-hood, and its replacement by its rightful Queen, the soul. Failure to practice these virtues strengthens the ego and increases our sense of separation from the universe and from God; successful practice weakens the ego and increases our awareness of the unity of all life under one holy Father. The practices of each of them is aimed at some crack in our armor that can be penetrated and then spread wide and then forced open, freeing us from the heavy burden of being ourselves. Of course, when that happens we do not become something else; we discover that which we had forgotten ages back: our own real Self, the Self of God, the Self of the universe,

4. Ajaib Singh, "Weed out Your Faults with Love," *Sant Bani,* May 1977, pp. 21-22

indisputably and undeniably our own all the same, our "original Face before we were born." It is through meditation that this happens, but the practice of the five virtues makes it possible; Kirpal Singh has described the relation between meditation and spiritual discipline (*sadhan* and *sadachar*) as the two wings of a bird.

Non-violence (*ahimsa*) or non-injury, like all the virtues, becomes possible to really practice when we are remembering God and our own origin. Remembering means that we will not be tricked into thinking that the person with whom we are becoming angry is other than ourselves. Anger also has a terrible disintegrating effect on the attention: after a violent outburst successful meditation becomes impossible, sometimes for many days. Another trick of the mind is to make us forget that: in the self-righteousness that almost always accompanies anger, we forget that the process of becoming angry and violent will do us more real harm by far than whatever it is we are getting angry about. When anger (or any of the "five dacoits"[5]) begin to conquer us, it does so by making us obsessed with the object or cause of the anger—whatever it is that is making us "mad"—so that we forget who it is that is becoming angry. Through practice of self-introspection, we gradually learn not to do this. It is a difficult job, especially for those who (like myself) have a short temper and are especially prone to getting angry; but it is a necessary job and, as long as we avoid morbidity and guilt when it dawns on us how much in control of these things we are and how little control we have when we are in the grip of them, it is a possible job. The practice of remembrance is really the only way to rise above any of these

5. The Masters refer to the opposites of the five virtues as the "five dacoits"—i.e., bandits or robbers, because they rob us of our attention. They are: lust, anger, greed, attachment, and ego.

failures, and that works much better as a prevention than a cure.

One aspect of non-violence that is readily in the grasp of anyone is the strict vegetarian diet which, as I have already mentioned, is a prerequisite for initiation and which was very difficult for me to accept in the beginning. It is very important to remember that the underlying reason for vegetarianism—the ultimate explanation of why eating flesh is responsible for bad karma and why it works against meditation—is the pain and fear and suffering that is caused fellow sentient beings by those who insist on eating them. No one should think that because he did not personally kill whoever it is that he is eating that he is not responsible for him. The person who eats the flesh of an animal is ultimately responsible for his death, because it is for him that it was done. If he both kills and eats him, so much the worse. The lives of our younger brothers and sisters count in the eyes of God; He made them too, and He loves them just as He loves us. They feel pain and fear and struggle to escape death just as we do. For human beings to put sense enjoyment or convenience or habit or whatever reason we have for continuing the practice of killing and eating others ahead of the very obvious reluctance of those others to die is a supreme victory of illusion; for there is nothing that binds us to the Karmic wheel of births and deaths tighter than this continual life-long slaughter. Kirpal Singh once quoted, "Thou shalt love thy neighbor as thyself," and then asked humbly, "Are these animals not your neighbors?"

Some people worry that they will not be healthy or strong or live long if they become vegetarians. This is groundless. The record of those people who have done it is clear and available. In our time Bernard Shaw and Mahatma Gandhi are notable examples of lifelong vegetarians. Shaw, one of the greatest writers and thinkers of the twentieth century, died at the age of 94. His last play, culminating a lifetime unmatched for productivity and vigorous fruitful contributions to the human treasury of wisdom, both in quantity and in quality, was written at the age of 90. Gandhi was murdered at the age of 78 in full strength and vigor while he was engaged in single-handedly trying to stop the rioting and civil war that was engulfing India at the time. These are just two examples involving the great and famous; there are hundreds more.

The careful investigator into these matters will not be surprised at this because he will already have discovered that physiologically the structure of human teeth, intestines, etc., are far better suited for vegetable food than for flesh. Striking verification of this is the fact that man's closest relatives in the Animal Kingdom—the anthropoid apes—are strict vegetarians by inclination and practice.[6] The gorilla, one of the strongest animals alive, whose physiological equipment is very close to man's, eats only vegetarian food from birth to death and fights only in self-defense. His supposed fierceness is in reality a projection of our qualities.

Economic considerations are also powerful: in a crowded and starving world it is fundamental morality to make the best use of the land at our disposal. It is a simple fact that the production of flesh food requires ten times as much land as the production of a comparable amount of vegetable food. Human survival may well depend on

6. One species of chimpanzee has in recent years learned to kill and eat flesh, thus re-enacting the history of human beings who presumably began killing during the last Ice Age. A fascinating study of human origins from a vegetarian point of view is Henry Bailey Stevens, *The Recovery of Culture.* For specifics on the land-use ratio of flesh vs. vegetarian food, see Frances Moore Lappe, *Diet for a Small Planet.*

whether we face up to this or not.

It is also relevant to say that vegetarianism, once the initial hurdle is gotten over, is really very easy. It has now been more than twenty years since I first became a vegetarian, and it was only in the first few years that I even *wanted* to eat meat. Eventually the desire for it drops completely away, and one would no more eat the flesh of animals, birds, or fish than he would the flesh of human beings—and for the same reasons.

The Masters lay great stress on this principle of non-violence, and it often comes as a shock to western minds to discover that a large number of them have spent some time—sometimes a lot of time—in the army.[7] There is really no inconsistency at all. The Masters see war as an evil, that's true; but they understand very well that in the world *as it is now constituted,* a strong army can be the most effective preserver of peace. The case of Switzerland is very persuasive: a small country surrounded by belligerent neighbors almost perpetually fighting each other, yet Switzerland has been at peace for six hundred years. While it is not wise to attribute this to any single reason, it is difficult not to think that her crack army, in which every able-bodied male is liable for service over a period of thirty years, has a lot to do with it. Historically, most wars have begun when a strong country thinks it can get away with attacking a weaker country. If the weaker country were not weaker, the war would not happen. Sawan Singh says in one of his letters, "If for the preservation of peace, he is to enlist as a soldier,

7. Of the four most recent Masters, Jaimal Singh was a professional soldier; Sawan Singh a military engineer and officer; Kirpal Singh served several months on "the firing line" as part of his career with the Indian equivalent of the Department of Defense; and Ajaib Singh served as an infantryman for ten years.

it is his duty to do so, for peace is a prelude to the practice of the Word."[8]

A careful study of the actions of Nazi Germany during the 1930's (not to mention imperialist Japan during the same period) will show the truth of it: because the Allied countries refused to see what was happening before their eyes, Hitler conquered Austria and Czechoslovakia with the greatest ease and had plenty of time to build up his army to where he thought he could conquer the world. He was wrong, of course; but how many lives were lost in the process of proving him wrong? A look at the map of Europe during the first few years of the war will show how close he came, and it was all needless. If only one of the Allied countries had been prepared to not wishfully think—if only one had cared enough about the innocent victims to protect them and stand up to the international bully when he was still vulnerable—how many millions of lives would have been saved?[9]

For no one should think that the practice of non-violence means standing aside and letting the strong prey on the weak. That is not non-violence, that is cowardice. A noble ideal is not enhanced by dressing it in ignoble garments. Only the brave can practice non-violence. Only he or she who is willing to protect others at the cost of his or her own life, if need be, can renounce the use of violence and use non-violent means whenever possible. We cannot renounce what we do not have.

2. Truthfulness (Satayam)

The Masters define a truthful person as one whose brain, heart, and tongue are in unison, and who consistently lives

8. Sant Bani, July 1978, p.25
9. See William Shirer, The Rise and Fall of the Third Reich.

up to his own highest vision; who earns his living honestly without being dependent on others; who does not interfere with others or attempt to manipulate them in order to fulfill purposes of his own; and who speaks that much of the truth which does not go to harm others. They advise us to think before we speak—"Is it true? Is it necessary? Is it kind?"—because the ideal of truthfulness should not be used as an excuse to judge or torment others.

It is very difficult to be consistently true to our own selves without the sustained and merciless practice of self-introspection, because the temptation to see our own actions in the best possible light and others' in the worst is almost impossible to resist. The habit of self-justification is very hard to break. It is probably safe to say that one who has examined himself and is not horrified by what he sees has not examined himself.

3. Chastity (Brahmcharya)

Probably none of the commandments of the Master is more difficult for people today to accept than the admonition to be chaste. The word itself is almost incomprehensible to us; we have forgotten what it means. Everyone knows that the most heinous crime we can commit is to repress. Doctors, clergymen, psychologists, writers proclaim the gospel of self-indulgence, and that is one gospel that is easy to believe. I also used to believe it, and in fact I resented the idea of chastity terribly when I first learned that it was part of the Master's teachings. But I found out the hard way that sexual indulgence is incompatible with meditation. The two cannot co-exist.

Physiologically, it is because of the *ojas,* the supra-physical substance that is manufactured by the body when orgasm does not take place. This *ojas* is known to yogis of all schools, and it makes possible the transfer of energy from the physical to the astral so that transcension of the body can take place. Without *ojas* there is no withdrawal and no rising above. Without chastity there is no *ojas*.

Morally, the Masters point out what is obviously a universal law of nature—that the sexual impulse is for the purpose of procreation and preservation of the species. When used for this purpose, there can be no objection to it. From the lowest form to the highest form, every kind of animal life known to us copulates only for the purpose of having young. In all other forms of animal life, the female is only desirable to the male when she is capable of bearing children. The male is aroused by the female only by her fertility. Apart from fertility there is no sex. Only human beings are the exception to this. Is there not food for thought in this—that perhaps there is something terribly wrong with man, of which this is a major symptom? If we looked at this phenomenon with an objective eye, what conclusion would we come to? What conclusion could we come to?

According to the Saints, "love" and "lust" are opposites; people in general dispute this, treating them as overlapping synonyms (as in the phrase, "making love"). But a careful examination shows that the Saints are right: that while it may be possible to "love" and to "lust after" the same person, the two have nothing to do with each other and do not usually coexist simultaneously. "Love" demands that the "other" be seen as a person, as a child of God whose needs, fears and hopes are of infinite value, whose personhood is of the first importance and can never be forgotten. Is this the way we look on others when we are in the grip of sexual desire? "Lust" demands in fact the exact opposite of this: that *our* needs are of infinite value and that the other be seen as a means to achieve them. Persons cease to be persons and are seen only as desire objects, and our primary relationship is not one of giving to them and respecting them as children of God, but of exploiting them and manipulating them to suit our needs.

Certainly the institution of marriage has done a great deal to contain lust, to build a fence of love and mutual respect around it. This is why marriage was introduced in the first place by the Rishis and law-givers of ancient times, and why the Masters lay so much stress upon it today. The impulse for sexual desire, placed in all species for the purpose of self-preservation, has gone berserk in man and like a mountain stream in springtime has far overflowed its banks and is engulfing everything else. Since the karma for exploiting others for our pleasure is very heavy, and the karmic connections with those with whom we have sexual intercourse labyrinthine, marriage was introduced as an arena, in which men and women could work through their sexual impulses, take the responsibility for the results of their actions by loving and raising their children, and learn to focus their relationship on mutual giving rather than mutual exploiting. If the man and woman are both seeking God they can transcend even the personal love they develop for each other by learning in the course of time Who it is that they are ultimately loving. Through the practice of Shabd Yoga, the sexual impulse gradually becomes weaker and desire recedes like a stream in the dry season. In this way a married couple can help each other to find God.

Kirpal Singh, speaking of chastity, has said:

"For that, the only criterion or specific remedy is what? To be Self-centered.[10] It is we who give power to the mind.

10. Obviously the Master does not mean that we are to be ego-

It is we who give power to the outgoing faculties. It is we who see good or bad outside. If we become Self-centered, we may make . . . use of our outgoing faculties however we like. At the present time, we are driven away, attracted by outside things. . . . If you are Self-centered and somebody touches you, you will not be affected. . . . The whole thing will depend on being Self-centered, to get your attention centered within you."[11]

Sexuality can be addictive in two ways, positive and negative. The positive addiction, which is by far the most prevalent in the world today, is straightforward enough and has been discussed above. The negative addiction often afflicts those who are trying to be chaste, or who consider themselves chaste, and is what is often called *repression*. Chastity is not repression. This must be grasped at once, or hopeless confusion results. Repression and sexual indulgence are the two sides of the coin of desire. A chaste person is neither repressed nor sensual; he is functioning on another level, and these points of reference have little meaning for him. A person who is addicted to heroin, for instance, is either giving in to his addiction or fighting it with all his might; a person who is not addicted is doing neither. Similarly, a chaste person is one who is free from desire except when he wishes to make use of it for the purpose for which it was intended. Such a person sees people of the opposite sex as children of God, not objects of desire. Such a person relates to other people so as to bring out their own latent divinity, not in such a way as to provoke their sexuality.

---

centered, which is what this term usually means. He is referring to the higher Self—the Atman.

11. Kirpal Singh, *Morning Talks,* p. 65

The Masters explain that, without forgetting the ultimate ideal of chastity, a young initiated married couple, faithful to one another and having one or two children, can, by keeping the vegetarian diet, practicing self-introspection, and feeding on the Light and Sound within, gradually outgrow the addiction to sex and eventually, without repression or dishonesty, see things in their true perspective and realize for themselves that that deep hunger which underlies our obsession with sexuality is not for sense pleasure or sensual fulfillment, but is on an infinitely deeper level and ultimately can be satisfied only by the union of our essence with its source.

It is very important, however, to understand that the Masters teach that the most important job of a married couple, and a necessary prelude to the attainment of chastity, is *to stay married to each other.* A chaste life is an ideal to work for and to lovingly help each other to attain, but if we are married it cannot be done unilaterally. It is up to each of us to promote the ideal in such a way that it is accomplished without inflicting pain or fear on our partner, and without causing the slightest strain in the fabric of our marriage.

4. Universal Love (Prem)

Unlike chastity, love is in good repute today but usually among those who do not know its price. In reality, love is every bit as hard to practice as is chastity and demands just as much awareness and remembrance. The truth of the matter is that love is chastity extended into areas of life other than the physical or sexual. Awareness of others as important in their own right, not because they relate either positively or negatively to our demands and goals; sensitivity to the needs and fears and suffering of others rather than demanding that they be sensitive to our needs and fears and sufferings; taking seriously Jesus's admonition and warning, "Judge not, lest ye be judged and found wanting"—this is what love costs. Ultimately the only way to pay that price is to rise to a place where we can see clearly that we can love our neighbor as ourself because he *is* ourself. And as Jesus indicated, love of God comes first. It is through the love of the Origin, of the Father, that we learn to love that which proceeded from the Origin—the children of the Father.

But loving God is hard. Who or what is "God" that we may love Him? What does He mean to us? Whatever mental picture we have of Him is unlike all others in that it is our own, with no basis in objective fact whatever. But if indeed He could make Himself known through some human being who had sacrificed his ego to such an extent that He could work through him—then there might be Someone to love Who was not just of our own make, Who had a real objective existence apart from our fantasy. Is this not the central fact of Christianity—that God has done just this? Are we then to assume that God is so limited, so sparing in His grace, that He would only do it once in the whole history of the world? Only a little common sense is needed to demonstrate that if He incarnated once through a human being for this purpose, He would do it again and again and again—because only the generation alive at the time can be benefited this way. Clement of Alexandria, one of the Fathers of the Church, wrote, "The Word became flesh so that man might learn from man how man becomes God." That's true—but if the Word does not continue to become flesh, then only a very few derive benefit, and the loving Father is partial indeed.

Swami Ji Maharaj of Agra said, a hundred years ago, "The Satguru is an incarnation eternally existent upon the earth." It is so. There is one Word, "the only begotten of the Father, full of grace and truth"; and that Word, Who is the one true only begotten Son, works through one human pole after another and makes Himself available to us—to love, to rejoice in, to thank God for—and above all so that we might, in loving the Son Who is clearly part of our experience, love the Father also.

This is why Sant Mat lays so much emphasis on *gurubhakti*, or love of the Master, and this is how the first and greatest commandment is made a practical reality; and it is the road to the realization of the second commandment too—the one that "is like unto" the first—because at bottom it is the same as the first. To love the Father is to love the children, and to love the Son is to love the Father. Distinctions are man-made and rooted in the duality and *maya* of the lower planes: when we reach Sach Khand we see very clearly that the Father, the Son, and all His children—including even us—are one—although the Masters are careful to point out that the souls who reach that far never make the intellectual monist mistake of assuming that they are thereby *equal* to God. They quote the great Hindu monist and mystic Shankara: "O God, there is no difference between Thee and me; nevertheless, I am Thine, Thou art not mine: because the wave can be of the ocean, but the ocean cannot be of the wave."

5. *Selfless Service* (Nishkam Seva)

If chastity and love are two facets of one attitude toward ourselves, toward others, and toward the universe, then a life of service is the expression or manifestation of that attitude. Service is to love as words are to thoughts. While it may not be necessary to deliberately seek out spectacular or interesting ways to serve, the fact is that if we keep our eyes open and become aware of and sensitive to the sufferings of others (as described above) we will find hundreds of ways to serve without altering the external necessities of our life at all.

The Masters say that there are a number of types of service, but two—physical and financial—are considered the most important. Let us examine these two carefully and try to understand what the Masters expect of us.

Physical Service: To make use of our body in the service of others is the highest use we can make of it. Selfless service physically has many aspects but, like the love of which they are all expressions, these aspects all go to weaken our ego and sense of separateness and strengthen our soul and sense of oneness.

"Naturally enough from love spring forth the ideas of service and sacrifice. Love believes in giving—giving away the best you have and not accepting anything in return, for that would be a barter and not love. 'Service before self' is what love teaches. *By love serve one another*, is what the Apostle Paul taught the Galatians, and through them to all mankind. If we look critically, we will soon realize that all service which we seem to be doing to others is not to anybody else, but to the ONE SELF-SAME SELF, pervading everywhere and in all, including our seemingly individualized self clothed in raiments of flesh and bones. This being the case, there is no ground for claiming any credit whatever. Loving service must therefore flow freely, fully and naturally, as a matter of course, refreshing all hearts, for it will convert the otherwise dreary and desolate earth into a veritable garden of Eden; for which we so earnestly pray every day but find it receding from us, the more we wish for it."[12]

12. Kirpal Singh, *The Way of the Saints*, pp. 352-3.

The idea of physical service includes also direct service to the Master, should the opportunity arise for the disciple to do it; but the highest form of service to the Master, as all Masters have explained, is for the disciple to "tithe his time" and devote at least two and a half hours each day to his spiritual practices.

Financial Service: The Masters also recommend the ancient practice of tithing money, suggesting that each disciple give one tenth of his income to some worthy cause or to individuals whom he knows need it. This is not entirely for the sake of the recipient. Kirpal Singh used to tell this story:

"Our Master (Sawan Singh) used to go to Baba Kahan[13] . . . When he went there he always gave Baba Kahan some . . . ten rupees. One time when Master was in the field area, he earned much money. He had a great amount of money, and when he went there he gave him the same ten rupees. Baba Kahan told him, 'Look here! You have earned so much money and you are giving me only ten? Haven't you any more?'—'Yes, I earned some more.'—'All right. I want much more.' Then Master told him, 'You have become greedy.'

"And what did Baba Kahan say? 'No, no. You see, if you leave it here, someone else will take it away. I am not to use it. My purpose is this: Whenever you are doing your duty, you are not doing it very honestly; sometimes you waste a few minutes—sometimes in talking or gossiping about something. Whatever you have not been very honest in doing as your duty, that percentage should be taken out of your income and must be sent for the good of others—to

13. A sadhu whom both Sawan Singh and Kirpal Singh used to visit before they met their Masters.

give to the poor, to the needy—so that your income will be all pure.'

"So earn your money, stand on your own legs and share with others. . . . After all, everything will remain here, whether you have hundreds or thousands or millions of dollars. Of course, the way you have earned the money, that will go along with you. . . ."[14]

Kirpal Singh used to quote Guru Nanak: "Truth is above all, but higher still is true living." It is because true living is the natural expression of a truthful heart that this is so. If truth as such does not express itself in true living then, according to Jesus, the heart is not truthful:

"Do men gather grapes of thorns or figs of thistles? Even so every good tree bringeth forth good fruit; but a corrupt tree bringeth forth evil fruit. A good tree cannot bring forth evil fruit, neither can a corrupt tree bring forth good fruit. . . . Wherefore by their fruits ye shall know them."[15]

The self-introspection diary, if kept as accurately and honestly and carefully as one can, serves as a kind of road-map of our inner progress or lack of it. If we notice that we are lost or on the wrong road, we stop our car, pull out the map, study it carefully, and when we have discovered where we went wrong, we turn the car around and go back to where we can find the right road. We do not, most of us, waste time crying and moaning and blaming ourselves and feeling guilty or morbid over the fact of getting lost. It is exactly the same with the self-introspection diary. If we use it properly, it is a marvelous guide that can show us exactly

14. From a talk given January 25, 1964 ("Living Up to It") published in *Sat Sandesh,* November 1976.

15. Matthew 7: 15-18, 20

where we went astray. If we use it as an excuse for morbidity, despair and guilt, we will profit nothing. The choice is ours.

CHAPTER SIX

Spiritual Meditation

While spiritual discipline as expressed in the observance of the five cardinal virtues and the practice of self-introspection is absolutely necessary on the spiritual path, and does lead to the attainment of inner peace, its relation to the ultimate aim of finding and seeing and becoming one with God is that of an elementary step. The primary means is what is called "meditation." Without spiritual discipline, meditation will not work, but without meditation it is not possible to go within. Of all that is required on the path of the Masters, meditation is the essence.

What is "meditation"? It is on every count to be regretted that the English word "meditation" means "thinking things over," because what one does when one "meditates" in this sense is precisely the opposite of that: it is the absence of thought. "Contemplation" is better, but that only describes one aspect. Perhaps the best term is "spiritual practices," a translation of the Sanskrit *sadhna* or Hindi *sadhan*. There are three of these practices: *Simran*, repetition or remembrance; *Dhyan,* contemplation or seeing the inner Light; and *Bhajan,* hearing the inner music or Sound Current. Each of the three has its own value and the practice of Surat Shabd Yoga involves all three. Each has its own fulfillment or completion, but the ultimate aim of the practice as a whole is union with the Positive Power or Supreme Father.

The way in which the three practices converge in

221

transcension of the physical plane and discovery of our own higher Self is described by Kirpal Singh in this way:

"The seat of the soul is between and behind the eyebrows. . . . It is at this point that the *sadhak* (practitioner) having closed his eyes must focus his attention, but the effort at concentration must be an effortless one and there must be no question of any physical or mental strain. To assist this effort the teacher gives the disciple a *mantra*, or charged verbal formula, which is symbolic of the journey ahead. This formula, when repeated slowly and lovingly with the tongue of thought, helps the disciple to collect his scattered thoughts gradually at a single point. What gives this mantra its potency is not any magic inherent in the words per se, but the fact that it is given by one who, by his own spiritual practice and mastery, has charged it with inner power. When the aspirant, by his inner concentration and by the mental repetition of the charged words, has brought his inward gaze to a sharp and steady focus, he will find that the darkness within that he at first confronted, gets gradually illuminated by shifting points of light. As his powers of concentration increase, the lights cease flickering and develop into a single radiating point.

"This process of concentration, or the collection of *surat*, automatically draws the spirit-currents, normally dissipated all over the body, toward the spiritual center. This withdrawal is greatly assisted by *simran* or repetition of the charged mantra; and the perception of the inner light, leading to *dhyan* or one-pointed concentration, quickens the process still further. In turn, dhyan when fully developed, leads to *bhajan* or inner hearing. The inner light begins to become resonant.

Within thee is Light and within the Light the
Sound, and the same shall keep thee attached to
the True One.

GURBANI

"The practitioner, when he shuts his physical ears, gets rapidly absorbed into the music. It is a common experience that though light can catch the eye, it cannot hold it for very long and has no very magnetic quality about it. But with music it is different. He who hears it in silence and stillness, is drawn irresistibly, as it were, into another world, a different realm of experience. And so the process of withdrawal that begins with *Simran* is stimulated by *Dhyan*, and is rapidly extended by *Bhajan*. The spiritual currents, already moving slowly, are carried upward, collecting finally at the third eye—the seat of the soul. The spiritual transcending of physical consciousness, or death in life, is thus achieved with the minimum of effort and travail.

"When students of the other forms of yoga reach the state of full physical transcendence after a long and exacting mastery of the lower chakras, they generally assume that they have reached their journey's end. The inner plane at which they find themselves—the realm of *Sahasrar* or *Sahasdal Kamal*, often symbolised by the sun-wheel, the lotus or the multifoliate rose—is indeed incomparably more beautiful than anything on earth, and in comparison appears timeless. But when the student of the Surat Shabd Yoga succeeds in rising above physical consciousness, he finds the Radiant Form of his Master waiting unsought to receive him. Indeed it is at this point that the real *Guru-shishya* or teacher-student relationship is established. Up to this stage, the Guru had been little more than a human teacher, but now he is seen as the divine guide or *Gurudev*, who shows the inner way:

*The feet of my Master have been manifested in
    my forehead,
And all my wanderings and tribulations have
    ended.*
                                    GURU ARJAN

*With the appearance of the Radiant Form of the
    Master within,
No secret remains hidden in the womb of time.*

"Christ also speaks in the same strain:

*There is nothing covered, that shall not be re-
    vealed, and hid, that shall not be known.*
                                    ST. MATTHEW

"Under the guidance of this Celestial Guide the soul learns
to overcome the first shock of joy, and realizes that its goal
lies still far ahead. Accompanied by the Radiant Form and
drawn by the Audible Life Current, it traverses from region
to region, from plane to plane, dropping off *kosha* after
kosha, until at last it stands wholly divested of all that is not
of its nature. Thus disentangled and purified it can at last
enter the realm where it sees that it is of the same essence as
the Supreme Being, that the Master in His Radiant Form
and the soul are not separate but One, and that there is
naught but the Great Ocean of Consciousness, of Love, of
Bliss ineffable. Who shall describe the splendour of this
realm?

*Only heart to heart can speak of the bliss of
    mystic knowers:
No message can tell it and no missive bear it.*
                                    HAFIZ

When the pen set to picturing this station,
It broke in pieces and the page was torn.

PERSIAN MYSTIC

"Having reached the journey's end, the seeker too merges with the Word and enters the company of the Free Ones. He may continue to live like other men in this world of human beings, but his spirit knows no limitations and is as infinite as God Himself. The wheel of transmigration can no longer affect him, and his consciousness knows no restrictions. Like his Master before him, he has become a Conscious Co-worker of the Divine Plan. He does nothing for himself but works in God's name. If there be indeed any *Neh-Karmi* (one free from the bonds of action), it is he, for there is no more potent means to freedom that the Power of the Word.

> *He alone is action-free who communes with the*
> *Word.*

GURBANI

"Freedom for him is not something that comes after death *(videh-mukti)*; it is something achieved in life itself. He is a *jivan-mukta* (free-in-life); like a flower shedding fragrance, he spreads the message of freedom wherever he goes.

> *Those who have communed with the Word, their*
> *toils shall end.*
> *And their faces shall flame with glory.*
> *Not only shall they have salvation,*
> *O Nanak, but many more shall find freedom with*
> *them.*

JAP JI

"In actual practice of the spiritual discipline, stress is laid on *Simran*, *Dhyan* and *Bhajan*, each of which plays a specific role in unfoldment of the Self. The Master gives

Simran or mental repetition of the charged words, which help in gathering together the wandering wits of the practitioner to the still point of the soul between and behind the two eyebrows, to which place the sensory currents now pervading from top to toe are withdrawn, and one becomes lost to the consciousness of the flesh. The successful completion of this process of itself leads to *dhyan* or concentration. *Dhyan* is derived from the Sanskrit root *dhi*, meaning 'to bind' and 'to hold on.' With the inner eye opened, the aspirant now sees shimmering streaks of heaven's light within him and this keeps his attention anchored. Gradually, the light grows steady in his sadhna, for it works as a sheet anchor for the soul. *Dhyan* or concentration when perfected, leads one to *Bhajan* or attuning to the music which emerges from within the center of the holy light. This enchanting holy melody has a magnetic pull which is irresistible, and the soul cannot but follow it to the spiritual source from whence the music emerges. The soul is helped by this triple process to slide out of the shackles of the body and becomes anchored in the heavenly radiance of its Self *(atman)*, and is led on to the heavenly home of the Father.''[1]

1. Kirpal Singh, *The Crown of Life*, pp. 155-160.

CHAPTER SEVEN

Self-Surrender

With each chapter the writing of this book has grown pro-
gressively harder. The simple narrative of my meetings with
Kirpal Singh and Ajaib Singh was one thing; the discussion
and explanation of their teachings was quite another. With
each new subject I have grown more conscious of a lack of
competence; and now with the final and cumulative chapter
this consciousness has also become climactic. The Master
told me to end the book this way, and I am doing it; but the
truth is that I know nothing about self-surrender because I
have never done it. It is true that I have occasionally reluctantly obeyed when my mind and senses were screaming at
me not to, and I suppose that in some technical sense that
was indeed surrender. But surrender as I understand the
term—the conscious and joyful recognition that God,
working through the living Master, is more competent and
benevolent regarding our life than our ego is, and the
deliberate "giving up" or "handing over" of our life to
Him with the consequent cessation of anxiety—this I have
never done.

Kirpal Singh writes about surrender in this way:

"Surrender to the feet of the Master means to merge
one's individual will in the will of the Master, and to completely place oneself at his mercy. It is the surest and easiest
way to escape from all cares and anxieties. It comes only
when a disciple has complete faith and confidence in the
competency of the Master.

"This type of self-surrender is like that of a completely helpless patient who, trusting in the skill of a competent surgeon, places his life in his hands and quietly submits himself to his knife and lancet.

"Or it may be compared to the trust given to the hopelessly lost traveler in the wilderness to the forest ranger who finds him and leads him out.

". . . an aspirant for spirituality has, after careful investigation, to decide first about the spiritual worthiness of a Master, and then to submit himself wholly and solely to his authority and direction without any mental reservations whatever; for he alone knows the turns and twists of the spiritual path and is in a position to act as an unerring guide. . . .

"In this context, we have the testimony of Hafiz, a great Sufi poet of Persia, who declared:

> *Dye thy prayer carpet in wine should the Master*
> *so desire;*
> *For he is not ignorant of the turns of the highway*
> *ahead.*"[1]

A remarkable story lying behind the couplet of Hafiz just quoted is told by Ajaib Singh in this way:

"Maharaj Sawan Singh used to tell one story about a Muslim Fakir in order to explain to us that we should always take the words of Master to our heart and we should always obey them no matter what. He used to say that there was one Muslim Fakir who gave out one sentence: 'If the Master wants you to wash your prayer mat in wine you should not hesitate to do that.' When that Muslim Fakir said this there was one *kazi* (priest), who came to him and

1. Kirpal Singh, *Godman*, pp. 177-179.

said, 'This is not according to the law of our religion! It is a very bad thing to wash the prayer mat in wine, and this is a bad thing for you to say. Explain to me why you say this.' That Muslim Fakir replied, 'Well, I can't tell you anything more about this, but you go to such-and-such a place where lives one of my disciples. Ask him and he will tell you what this line means.' So that Kazi went to the disciple of the Fakir and asked him, 'Your Master has made this statement: that if Master wants, you should even wash your prayer mat in wine, and you should not hesitate to do it. Please tell me, why did your Master make this statement? What is the meaning of this?'

"That disciple said, 'I cannot give you any reply to this. But if you want to get the reply, you should go to a certain town (he mentioned its name), and there you will find one prostitute. You go to her and ask her and she will tell you. And in that way you will know the meaning of this sentence said by the Master.' The Kazi was confused and said, 'What type of Fakirs are they? One says that you should wash the prayer mat in wine; the other says you should go to a prostitute.' He was confused, but he was intelligent and he thought, 'Let me go and see what is happening with the prostitute.' He went to her house but she was not there.

"The people who were there thought, 'He looks like a good man; let us present a new girl to him so that he will give us more money.' In the house of the prostitute there lived a young girl, who had been sold by some bandits to that prostitute and had been brought up by her. They presented that girl to the Kazi, thinking that he would give them a lot of money. This was the first time that the girl had been presented to any man. She was very shy and started weeping when she came into the room where the Kazi was sitting. The Kazi thought, 'If she is a prostitute she should have just come to me and welcomed me and loved me and things like that; there is some secret behind it. Let me ask her who she is and why she is feeling shy.' So he asked her, 'Tell me what is wrong with you and why you are crying?' The girl replied, 'Up until now I have been innocent; I have not had to face any man. But I am separated from my family and my father and I am afraid that today I am stepping into hell, and I don't know how I will be punished by God. That's why I am afraid and I am crying.'

"That Kazi, who was a religious man, felt pity for her and asked her about her family. She replied that during the revolution she had been separated from her family. When the Kazi heard that, he at once remembered his family because he was also ruined in the same revolution. He asked her, 'What was the name of your village? So she replied, 'I don't know exactly but it was something like this . . .' She mentioned some name, and that was the very village of the Kazi. When he realized that she was from his village his curiosity increased more and more and he got the courage to ask her more about her family and herself. So then he asked her, 'Do you remember what the name of your father was?' She said, 'I don't remember exactly but I think it was like this . . .' and it was exactly the name of the Kazi. So in that way the Kazi and his daughter were reunited after a long separation.

"So then the Kazi realized that that was the meaning of the statement: that whatever Saints say, you should just go ahead and do it, no matter what it means at the moment; whatever they say, it is good for you. He got his daughter and when he came back to the Muslim Fakir, he requested him to say the other half of the couplet. He said to the Fakir, 'Now I understand what you meant: that we should not hesitate in following the commandments no matter what He says. Now please tell me the other half of the couplet.' Then the Muslim Fakir finished the couplet and said: 'Whatever statement the Master makes, even if you think it goes against the teachings of the Masters, still you should do it; because Master is all-conscious and He knows what you want.' He has his own way of explaining things to you. That's why you should never hesitate in obeying the commandments of the Master, no matter in what way they are presented to you. You should always go ahead and do whatever He wants you to do. Whatever He utters from His mouth is good for you."[2]

The psychological reasons for self-surrender, and how it fits into the framework of the spiritual teachings as a whole, is explained by Kirpal Singh in this way:

"You may well ask why there is this insistent stress on complete self-surrender on the mystic path. The answer is simple: without this absolute surrender of the last vestiges of ego and selfhood and without such complete absorption in the object of one's love, one cannot attain that unwavering concentration of all one's faculties which is the prerequisite of all inner progress. Absolute love and self-surrender are only other aspects of complete and flawless concentration. The moment the 'self' enters into the picture and the question of 'I-ness' arises, the single-pointedness of concentration is dissipated and inner advancement is made impossible. Besides, the goal of the spiritual aspirant lies far beyond the limits of individuality. His goal is union with the Absolute and such union must necessarily be a denial of the limits that separate us from each other. He who cannot rise above the ego, the faculty which creates these very limits,

2. *Sant Bani*, November 1978, pp. 4-5

cannot hope to attain to that station which is the denial of all individuality and a realization of the oneness of all life.

"Hence it is that mystics of all traditions have been untiring in their stress of the need for absolute self-surrender. It was this cross of sacrifice of the self, the ego, of which Jesus spoke when he exhorted his disciples to bear their cross daily. For in every little act, word or thought, the ego is seeking to dominate us and if the seeker is to triumph over it, he must be prepared to crucify it every moment. To achieve this degree of self-surrender, one must not look up to the Deity in its Abstract form but in its human form as the Master, who is attuned to the Lord and is His mouthpiece, and if he obeys Him in all things completely and absolutely, he will surely destroy the hydra-headed serpent of the ego and reach his heavenly home one day. There will be moments in the course of such love when one, judging from one's own limited understanding, doubts the validity of the Master's instructions, but such moments are only tests to make our self-surrender more complete and secure, and he who passes through these tests successfully, will one day radiate with the glory of God."[3]

Even though implicit obedience is one of the fruits of surrender Kirpal Singh in one place differentiates between surrender and obedience:

"Self-surrender is not an easy task. To accomplish it, one has to recede back to the position of an innocent child. It means an entire involution, a complete metamorphosis, supplanting one's own individuality.

"It is the path of self-abnegation, which not everyone can take.

"On the other hand, the path of spiritual discipline is

3. Kirpal Singh, *The Way of the Saints*, pp. 308-310.

comparatively easy. Self-effort can be tried by anyone in order to achieve spiritual advancement.

"It is, no doubt a long and tortuous path, as compared with the way of self-surrender, but one can, with confidence in the Master, tread it firmly step by step. If, however, a person is fortunate enough to take to self-surrender, he can have all the blessings of the Master quickly, for he goes directly into his lap and has nothing to do by himself for himself."[4]

The usefulness of self-surrender as a means of undercutting the ego is obvious; and it has been advocated for this purpose by all past Masters. Jesus laid great stress on it, indicating that it was the most important act of all:

"And, behold, one came and said unto him, Good Master, what good thing shall I do, that I may have eternal life?

"And he said unto him, Why callest thou me good? There is none good but one, that is, God: but if thou wilt enter into life, keep the commandments.

"He saith unto him, Which? Jesus said, Thou shalt do no murder, Thou shalt not commit adultery, Thou shalt not steal, Thou shalt not bear false witness, Honor thy father and thy mother: and, Thou shalt love thy neighbor as thyself.

"The young man saith unto him, All these things have I kept from my youth up: what lack I yet?

"Jesus said unto him, If thou wilt be perfect, go and sell what thou hast, and give it to the poor, and thou shalt have treasure in heaven: and come and follow me."[5]

4. Kirpal Singh, *Godman,* pp. 180-181
5. Matthew 19: 16-21

The same demand is as familiar in the Zen tradition as in the Christian:

"The teachers succeed in putting their pupils through this apparently soul-less [Zen] discipline thanks to their astounding psychological experiences, for they themselves have travelled the same path; moreover, they have at their disposal the accumulated experience of centuries. Great Masters can do the most amazing things in this respect, sometimes bordering on the incredible. The pupil who doubts their capacity to see into every corner of his soul soon learns that his resistance, whether conscious or instinctive, is in vain. Naturally, the Oriental seldom finds himself in this position. Unstinting veneration of his teacher is in his blood; it is part of his tradition. For the Master gives him his best, which will also be the pupil's best—his best in a spiritual sense. This consists least of all in things of the intellect which can be detached from the original giver, leaving him forgotten, but in that wealth of spiritual power which only one who has experienced it possesses, and which—logically—is not his own.

"If the pupil is ever to have mystical experiences he will owe them solely to his teacher. For him the fate of his pupil is as important as his own fate; he is ready to sacrifice himself in the performance of his duty. Above all—and this must be especially emphasized—he always has time for his pupils.

"As a result, the relationship of the pupil to master is one of absolute confidence and unquestioning devotion. The master, on his side, accepts this gratitude, veneration, and love as something not due to him personally, for his power does not derive from himself and from what, through his own efforts, he has made of himself, but from the *unio*.

Consequently he sees in it no cause for self-satisfaction. But he does not forbid his pupil's devotion; he accepts it as inevitable so long as the pupil is dependent on his spiritual leadership and has not yet related himself to the center. Once this center is found, the relationship will no longer be one of faith and trust, but of knowledge.

"Anything the Master asks will be done by the pupil—not with the ostentatious assiduity of the religious careerist (all such soon drop out of the school), but from an inner impulse of dedication. This can be seen from the way pupils speak of the Master among themselves—with a kind of sacred awe. For them he is the model and prototype, and even their exceedingly sharp and discerning eyes can detect no fault in him, although they are constantly in his presence. The disaster, otherwise, would be total, for their whole world would collapse. And the Master, if he were conscious of even the smallest imperfection in himself, would voluntarily renounce his high office and cease to lead others. For on the long and self-abnegating path of Zen there are so many obstacles, disappointments and failures, that if the pupils could not put blind trust in the Master, and find this trust vindicated at all times, they would not be able to stay the course. This faith alone sustains them; not the conviction that they will reach the goal, but that the Master is leading them in the right direction—so far as it is their destiny to go. And should they have to break off before reaching the goal, they know that it is worth a whole life to have gone even that much of the way. What keeps them going is not direct faith in ultimately reaching the goal, for that is far off and as yet without effect. But it becomes effective through the Master; and thus faith in the Master is, indirectly, faith in the goal."[6]

6. Eugen Herrigel, *The Method of Zen,* pp. 24-27.

This comment, by a European who spent many years in Japan, is as complete and concise a statement on the problem as a whole that I have ever read. It is obvious that the practice of surrender to a Master will not work if the Master is not perfect—"perfect" here being defined among other things as perfectly and continually aware that the Power working through him is what the disciple is surrendering to, and not he himself. While the disciple cannot differentiate between the two practically (he may intellectually) the Master must, or he becomes a devil instead of a saint. It is of course incumbent on the disciple to be certain before he surrenders that the Master does indeed make that distinction and is not interested in self-aggrandizement.

This may seem like a difficult task. But in practice it is not. For one thing, as the first chapters of this book demonstrate, any genuine seeker will have help. If this were not so, then Jesus's promise ("Seek and ye shall find") would not make any sense. All people have a built-in sensor that alerts them as to whether or not the person they have come to can really help them. If however our search is not for the Truth, but is only an escape from responsibility, or a desire to find some wish-fulfillment figure, or any one of a number of other possibilities, it may not suit us to listen very closely to our built-in sensor and we can get badly messed up.

For another thing, there are some very simple clues which go a long way in helping us to decide whether or not someone is true or false. A true Guru is not interested in money, lives off his own earnings, and in no case accepts money for his own use from the disciples. Neither does he charge for any initiation or meditation lessons or lectures that he may give. He may accept voluntary offerings (neither he nor any responsible follower will ever put pressure on anyone to give, however) but if he does, they will either be distributed among the poor or used for the expenses of the work —travel expenses, feeding the people who come to his ashram, etc. This is a very clear-cut and obvious criterion which immediately eliminates the vast majority of gurus.

"The second is like unto it." Not only does a real Master not depend on his disciples financially, he doesn't depend on them physically or emotionally either. In the real guru-disciple relationship, it is the guru who gives and the disciple who takes. The Master does not need anybody; it is the disciples who need Him. He is here under orders for their sake, to give them what they need in order that they may do what he has done and accomplish what he has accomplished. He is not here to work out emotional or psychological problems or fantasies through his disciples. It goes without saying that a real Guru will not have such problems or fantasies and that the seeker will do well to make sure of this point before surrendering himself to anybody. There are a number of points that a seeker may watch for:

1) A real Master has a sense of humor, and he does not mind laughing at himself. He is not concerned with his "image" but lives in the living present and responds to the needs of the people he is with.

2) A real Master has no personal interest in having a large following; nor does he care, from a personal point of view, whether any individual disciple leaves him or not. He will not allow the use of pressure tactics or salesmanship—any method which impinges on the freedom of the seeker—either to win new disciples or to keep old ones.

3) Because of this, a real Master does not tell the disciple what he wants to hear, but what he needs to hear for the sake of his own growth. If the disciple is really after Truth, he will understand this and appreciate it; if he is not, he will

leave the Master and attach himself to some so-called guru who will know how to take advantage of him.

4) Kirpal Singh often quoted Jesus, "I have not come to make you slaves, but friends." A real Master is not a dictator, and surrender to Him is not something that can be or should be forced by Him. It is a voluntary gift rooted in love, from a lover to his Beloved. If the Master demands it as His personal due, there is something wrong. Kirpal Singh used to tell this story from His own life, before He met His Master:

"Naturally, when I looked all around, there were so many Masters. To whom should I go? We were three brothers. Two of us helped each other. 'If you find any Godman, tell me; if I find one, I will tell you.' We were searching, you see.

". . . Once, it so happened, that my brother wrote me, 'Here's a very great man; a very great Master has come. Will you come?' I went there. I told him, 'I have intoxication that continues day and night; but sometimes, after three, four or five months, it breaks for a day or two. And I am very much puzzled. Can you help me in that?'

"What did he say?—'You'll have to lay down everything —your body, mind and soul—to me. Only then I can, I will, give it to you.'

"I thought, 'The man is after my body and possessions; my intellect and everything is to be blindfolded.' I paid him homage and returned. Well, you see—surrender comes only when you see some competence. Devotion and love—one who loves—is something else. When you surrender, you have control of the one to whom you surrender: he has to take care of you.'"[7]

7. Kirpal Singh, "How I Met My Master," *Sat Sandesh,* July 1975, pp. 4-5

5) A real Master is humble, but His humility is of a different order than ours. It is probably safe to say that only real Masters are humble, as distinguished from trying to be humble: the Master's humility is not put on in an effort to convince others that He is indeed spiritual, but is based on His certain first-hand knowledge that He is not the doer, that it is the Power of God working through His Master that is responsible for everything—including the miraculous and wonderful things—that seem to us to be said or done by Him. A marvelous story is told of Baba Sawan Singh: at the age of 88, in July 1946, He took the mail train from Lahore to Karachi. (This was before the creation of Pakistan and both cities were then in India.) Both at the Lahore station, where He boarded the train, and at every station along the way, the platform was jammed with people who wanted to see Him. At each station He came out and gave a short talk. At Montgomery, where there was a large Satsang, the Satsangis put up a canopy and Baba Sawan Singh left the train and held Satsang at the station. At this station also the engine was discovered to have developed some defect, so that the train was delayed there for more than half an hour, to the delight of the Satsangis. At Khanewal and Multan the crowds were so big that it was difficult to move, and the Master gave His darshan at both places, the train waiting for Him to finish before moving. By this time the train was running several hours late, and everyone on board knew that a holy man was on the train.

At Tahim Yarkhan, the passengers learned that a freight train two miles ahead of them had had an accident and they would have to stay at that station for the night. What had happened was that some Muslim terrorists called *Hurs*, agitating for the creation of Pakistan, had removed the fish plates from the track hoping to sabotage the Karachi Mail (the train Baba Sawan Singh was traveling in) and in this way murder the thousands of passengers on board.

Because the Karachi Mail was so late, however, the freight train had received permission to go ahead of it and thus was derailed instead, with no loss of life at all. Both the passengers and townspeople were convinced that it was the presence of Sawan Singh on the train that had saved it, and it was demonstrably true: the train was saved because of its lateness, and the lateness was primarily due to the Master's presence. Cots were set up on the station platform for the passengers, and most of the leading citizens of the town spent the night there. In the morning, on request of the townspeople, the Master gave Satsang on the station platform, then talked to a continuous stream in His compartment on the train—all thanking and praising Him for having saved the train. He absolutely refused to accept their praise, saying, "I am an ordinary man, not a Mahatma or Saint, but a humble and sinful soul of God. God is as much in you as He is in me. There is no difference between us."

When the Satsangis who were present begged the Master to tell the truth about Himself and reveal Himself fully, He instead told them a story of Kabir: The pundits and other professional religionists were jealous of Kabir's popularity, so they proclaimed that on a certain day there would be a great *Bhandara* or feast at Kabir's house, and everyone was invited. Kabir was a poor man; how could He feed thousands of people? It was done to embarass Him. He hid in the jungle during the time of the feast and came back the next day. But from His hiding place He could hear the people leaving His house and praising the quality of the food they had been given, and when He returned home His family told Him that He had been there all along and had fed everybody. Kabir exclaimed: "Kabir has not done it, would not have done it, could not have done it; it is God Who has done it, and the credit has gone to Kabir." Baba Sawan Singh concluded that it was the same with Him, and that Saints always remain in the will of God.

Because the humility of the Saints comes from Their objective vision of Themselves, just as They refuse to take credit for what they have not done, so do They freely use incidents from Their own lives to illustrate attitudes or ways of behavior that They would like Their disciples to try to adopt. At first hearing this sort of thing might sound egotistical (Kirpal Singh, for instance, used to tell how, when He retired from government service, it took three men to replace Him, because He had managed His department so efficiently) but further reflection makes clear that He is simply viewing His life objectively, as He would anybody else's, and He is drawing upon it, whether good or bad, to help His disciples grow. There is a difference between humility and false modesty.

These are ways to get some indication of whether a Master is real or not, so that we will know, as much as we can, whether surrender to Him is a surrender to God or to somebody's ego. In the final analysis, however, no criterion really works infallibly, and we ultimately have to act according to the love that is in our hearts: it is a matter of being true to our own selves. Why? Because the Masters are free, and being free are unpredictable. Masters neither take drugs or intoxicants (including tobacco) Themselves nor allow Their disciples to do so; yet both Swami Ji Maharaj and Ramakrishna smoked the *hookah*. Masters generally set a good example to others and live up to what they say; yet Kabir and Ravidas once went through the streets of Kashi arm in arm, singing and drinking water out of wine bottles. There are many examples of this kind and they add up to this: that the seeker has got to pay attention to the love in his own heart and act according to that. Masters act in these difficult ways solely to force the seeker back into his own heart, so that no one will come to Them because they think they ought to, or because someone they know says they should, or because everybody else is doing it. When, after a long and difficult search over all of northern India, Baba Jaimal Singh found Swami Ji Maharaj, it was with a real jolt that He realized that His Guru was not a Sikh and that He smoked a hookah. But He still remained subject to the truth of His own search and took the initiation anyway. He went very far within and stayed there for two days; when He came out, Swami Ji asked Him with a smile, "Do you, my boy, still doubt if your Master be a true Sikh or not?" No one who is really and with a whole heart after the Truth, and who is true to his or her own self, to the love and longing that has been developed in his or her own heart by the grace of God, can be deceived for long. The great promise of Jesus with which this book began will also be its ending, and should never be forgotten by any seeker:

> *Seek and ye shall find; . . . he that seeketh findeth; to him that knocketh it shall be opened. Or what man is there of you, whom if his son ask bread, will he give him a stone? . . . If ye then, being evil, know how to give good gifts unto your children, how much more shall your Father which is in heaven give good things to them that ask him?*